Enumeration of Educable Children in Pontotoc County, Mississippi

1892

Hazel Boss Neet

HERITAGE BOOKS
2015

HERITAGE BOOKS
AN IMPRINT OF HERITAGE BOOKS, INC.

Books, CDs, and more—Worldwide

For our listing of thousands of titles see our website
at
www.HeritageBooks.com

Published 2015 by
HERITAGE BOOKS, INC.
Publishing Division
5810 Ruatan Street
Berwyn Heights, Md. 20740

Copyright © 2002 Hazel Boss Neet

Heritage Books by the author:
Enumeration of Educable Children in Pontotoc County, Mississippi, 1892
Enumeration of Educable Children in Pontotoc County, Mississippi, 1894
Pontotoc County, Mississippi, Marriage Book, 1849–1891

All rights reserved. No part of this book may be reproduced or transmitted in any form or by any means, electronic or mechanical, including photocopying, recording or by any information storage and retrieval system without written permission from the author, except for the inclusion of brief quotations in a review.

International Standard Book Numbers
Paperbound: 978-0-7884-2053-5
Clothbound: 978-0-7884-6243-6

THE FOLLOWING ARE THOSE WHO HAVE A GUARDIAN OR THEIR SURNAME IS DIFFERENT THAN THEIR PARENT. ALSO A LIST OF THOSE WHOSE PARENT OR GUARDIAN IS UNKNOWN. THEY MAY BE LOCATED ON THE PAGE GIVEN.

NAME	PAGE
Arnold, Miller	53
Baker, Chas	25
Baker, Will	25
Barnes, James	9
Barton, Robt	38
Bean, Geo	65
Beeson, Bettie	88
Beeson, Eula	88
Beeson, James	88
Beeson, Anna	88
Beeson, Emma	88
Beeson, Robt	88
Beeson, Malinda	88
Bell, Willie	111
Billingsley, Chas	79
Billingsley, Anna	79
Blakely, Hattie	58
Blackstock, Henry	76
Blackstock, Joe	76
Blackstock, Luster	76
Blackstock, Alice	76
Bolton, Pearl	5
Bolton, Etta	5
Bolton, Martha	82
Boothe, Wm	103
Boothe, James	103
Boothe, Mary	103
Brazile, Robt	83
Brazile, Ada	83
Brazile, Lizzie	83
Brazile, Maggie	83
Brown, Rubin	1
Buchellon, Harry	101
Burton, Robt	41
Caldwell, Lizzie	90
Cannon, Georgia	33
Cannon, Sam	79
Chatman, Perry	81
Chatman, Flora	81
Chatman, Etta	81
Collums, Jno	92
Collums, Sam	92
Cox, Ida	75
Cox, Dock	75
Cox, Jane	75
Crawford, Gus	102

NAME	PAGE
Cruse, Geo	47
Cruse, Maggie	60
Cruse, Ludie	31
Cummings, Anna	71
Cummings, Jno	71
Cypert, Maud	64
Cypert	64
Dees, Claudie	78
Dees, Henry	78
Dickerson, Ed	98
Dillard, Sam	6
Dillard, Malissa	6
Dillard, Sam	42
Douglas, Thos	21
Douglas, Nora	28
Duke, Thos	92
Duke, Robt	59
Duke, Luther	59
Duke, Sallie	59
Duke, Thos	59
Duke, Ella	59
Duke, Bettie	29
Duke, Lizzie	29
Duke, Oscar	29
Duke, Jas	29
Duke, Alf	29
Duke, Ed	9
Duke, Geo	9
Duke, Florence	9
Duncan, Geo	67
Dunevant, Maud	29
Duff, Boon	29
Duff, Albert	29
Durham, Jack	28
Durham, Susie	28
Edwards, Ben	99
Edwards, Jake	52
Eubanks, Will	104
Eubanks, Cal	104
Eubanks, Emma	104
Eubanks, Dock	104
Eubanks, Prestin	104
Eubanks, Daisy	104
Gillespie, Thos	81
Gillespie, Wm	81
Graham, Ed	72
Griffen, Lee	28
Griffen, Cora	28
Griffin, Chas	35
Griffin, Claudie	35
Griffin, Minnie	35

Gregory, Josie	55
Gregory, Joe	55
Gregory, Venus	55
Gregory, Ju	55
Gregory, Geo	55
Hamilton, Lawrence	42
Harden, Lizzie	69
Hardin, B.	39
Hare, Lela	115
Harris, Will	7
Herd, Thos	92
Herd, Peter	92
Herd, Hannah	92
Hitchcock, Bettie	55
Hodges, Ed	2
Hodges, Ida	2
Homan, Jno	17
Hooper, A.R.	51
Houpt, Bettie	9
Howard, Wes	51
Howard, Price	51
Howard, Frank	51
Howard, Joe	51
Hyde, Jas	112
Hyde, Addie	112
Hyde, Minor	112
Hyde, Antney	112
Johnson, Jim	90
Johnson, Robt	99
Joyner, David	113
Joyner, James	113
Joyner, Laura	113
Joyner, Burrell	113
Joyner, Dora	113
Knight, Lee	59
Leach, Nannie	1
Leach, Della	1
Leslie, Jack	32
Leslie, Ed	106
Leslie, Celia	106
Lindsay, Willie	2
Lindsay, Jno	2
Lindsay, Dab	2
Lindsay, Vallie	2
Luther, M.	51
Luther, Effie	51
McCraw, Mollie	89
McCraw, Burrah	89
McGuirt, Jno	31
McWhorter, Jas	53

NAME	PAGE
Mahan, Mart	105
Mayo, Judson	60
Mayo, Eva	60
Mayo, Katie	60
Miller, Blossie	2
Miller, Dan	85
Miller, Wes	85
Miller, Ben	85
Miller, Cora	85
Miller, Will	11
Montgomery, Maggie	112
Mormon, Lillie	35
Mullins, Minnie	79
Mullins, Nannie	79
Nabors, Jno	54
Nabors, Jeff	54
Nathan, Jo	51
Neal, Lou	65
Nolan, Savannah	14
Nolan, Lela	14
Nolan, Ida	14
Nolan, Fannie	14
Orr, Mattie	57
Owen, Mattie	6
Owen, Jno	6
Owen, Addie	92
Owen, Jno	92
Owen, Meloin	92
Palmer, Jno	98
Parrish, G.L.	71
Patterson, Josie	68
Payne, Henry	112
Phillips, Elena	106
Phillips, Egbert	106
Pinson, Mose	41
Pitts, Bee	49
Pitts, Nora	49
Pitts, Fred	41
Pope, Ed	49
Pope, Alma	49
Pope, Vardie	49
Porter, Rush	1
Prude, Cora	46
Prude, Nellie	107
Purdon, J.F.	99
Purdon, L.E.	99
Ramey, Mack	2
Ramey, Ira	2
Ridge, Harvy	79
Robbins, Isaac	93

NAME	PAGE
Roebuck, Dillard	95
Roebuck, Artway	95
Roebuck, Morgan	95
Roebuck, Cynthia	95
Roebuck, Manie	95
Rogers, Sarah	43
Rolan, Lou	85
Rolan, Dollie	85
Rolan, Carry	85
Rolan, John	85
Rolan, Gardner	85
Rutledge, Junior	66
Sadler, Henry	21
Shannon, Rob	51
Smith, Enoch	81
Smith, M.E.	115
Smith, S.E.	115
Smith, Willie	113
Smith, Joe	113
Souter, Clara	27
Souter, Clara	27
Staten, Robt	25
Stevens, Ed	104
Stevens, Sallie	104
Todd, Ben	39
Todd, Julia	39
Todd, Abe	39
Vance, S.	104
Vance, S.	79
Waldo, Pearl	13
Waldo, Cora	13
Waldo, Chester	13
Walker, Thos	22
Ware, Rhoda	104
Ware, Thos	104
Ware, Harrison	104
Ware, Wm	104
Warren, Minnie	105
Warren, Dillie	105
Warren, Cordie	105
Warren, Martin	105
Warren, Lizzie	105
Warren, Immer	105
Westmoland, Burrell	72
Wheeler, Callie	104
White, Ed	110
Wilder, Emma	70
Wilder, Lester	86
Williams, Lena	69
Williams, Geo	69
Williams, Ol	51

NAME	PAGE
Wilson, Clifton	42
Woods, Willie	70
Wysinger, Ed	55

UNKNOWN PARENT OR GUARDIAN

NAME	PAGE
Pitts, Robt	101
Suggs, Hattie	101
Suggs, Jno	101
Suggs, Bulah	101
Vickerson, Booker	101
Rucker, Thos	101
Bryon, Henry	101

1892 PONTOTOC, MISSISSIPPI SCHOOL CENSUS

Only the parent or guardian name was given with the children between the ages of five and twenty-one and the color. No other information recorded. There are some duplications, but note the difference in the Range and Township - so apparently the family moved before the census was completed.

Aaron, Dan - Range 1, Township 10 - White
   Sam - female, age 10   Jno - male, age 7
   Chas. - male 4, age 8   Harrison - male, age 5

Aaron, J.D. - Range 1, Township 10 - White
   Julia - female age 14   Lee - male, age 9
   Alfred - male, age 11   Barney - male, age 6

Abbott, Ira - Range 4, Township 9 - White
   Mary - female, age 16   Walter - male, age 6
   Nannie - female, age 13

Abernethy, J.R. - Range 4, Township 11 - White
   Ed - male, age 17   Lester - male age 10
   Anna - female, age 15   Mary, female, age 5

Abernethy, R.B. - Range 4, Township 11 - White
   Ed - male 17   Willie - male age 11
   Mamie - female, age 14   Bettie - female, age 9

Abernethy, W.J. - Range 3, Township 11 - White
   Wm - male, age 20   M.E. - female, age 14
   Jas. - male, age 18   Anna - female, age 12
   B.S. - male, age 16   Jno - male, age 8

Abney, F.S. - Toccopola - White
   Max - male, age 6

Adams, A. - Range 1, Township 10 - White
   Willis - male, age 12   Alice - female, age 10
   Lizzie - female, age 13   Mamie - female, age 6

Adams, J.E. - Range 1, Township 11 - White
   Loyd - male, age 5

Adams, W.T. - Range 1, Township 11 - White
   Florence - female 6   Lillie - female, age 11

Alexander, B. - Guardian - Range 4, Township 9 - White
   Brown, Rubin - male age 10   Leach, Della - female, age 8
   Leach, Nannie

Alexander, C. - Range 1, Township 9 - Colored
   Henrietta - female, age 19   Howard - male, age 15
   Robt - male, age 20

Alexander, Jack - Range 2, Township 10 - Colored
   Carson - male, age 7

Allen, G.W. - Range 2, Township 8 - Colored
   Lizzie - female, ge 18   Mollie - female, age 17
   Geo - male, age 18   Rass - female, age 11
   Mollie - female, age 17   Hattie - female, age 9

Alsup, Mrs. E. - Guardian - Range 1, Township - White
   Porter, Rush - male, age 6

Anderson, B.D. - Pontotoc - White
    Delffie - female, age 13   Lindsay, Dab - male, age 7
    Lindsay, Willie - male age 11   Lindsay, Vallie - female, age 5
    Lindsay, Jno - male, age 9   Miller, Blossie - female, age 16

Anderson, B.F. - Range 1, Township 10 - White
    Josie - female, age 14   Ivy - male, age 6
    Richard - male, age 10

Anderson, B.F. - Guardian - Range 1, Township 10 - White
    Hodges, Ed - male, age 19
    Hodges, Ida - female, age 18

Anderson, G.M. - Range 4, Township 8 - White
    Geo - male, age 7   Dick - male, age 6

Anderson, G.T. - Range 1, Township 10 - White
    Martha - female, age 18   Bettie - female, age 10
    Nathaniel - male, age 17   Jno - male, age 8
    Geo - male, age 15

Anderson, J.P. - Range 1, Township 10 - White
    Dickey - female, age 17   Lum - male, age 12

Anderson, J.P. - Guardian - Range 1, Township 10 - White
    Ramey, Mack - male, age 10   Ramey, Ira - female, age 6

Anderson, J.Q. - Range 1, Township 10 - White
    Henry - male, age 20   Joe - male, age 11
    Geo - male, age 19   Jessee - male, age 8
    Colonel - male, age 13

Anderson, P.M. - Range 4, Township 9 - White
    Vannie - female, age 18   Mabel - female, age 13
    Frances - female, age 16

Andrews, M. - Range 2, Township 8 - White
    Narcissa - female, age 17   Claud - male, age 8

Andrews, Sallie - Range 2, Township 9 - White
    Cora - female, age 8

Angle, J.E. - Range 3, Township 11 - White
    Thos - male, age 16   Buffalo - male, age 8
    Emma - female, age 14   Lewis - male, age 6
    Jno - male, age 12

Archer, Dave - Range 4, Township 11 - White
    Martha - female, age 15   Jo - male, age 11
    Wm - male, age 13   Cleveland - male, age 6

Archer, Joe - Range 4, Township 10 - White
    Mat - male, age 18   Willie - male, age 12
    Hattie - female, age 14

Ard, Geo - Range 2, Township 10 - White
    Dora - female, age 13   Chas - male, age 9
    Ida - female, age 11   Maggie - female, age 7
    Wm - male, age 10   Mary - female, age 5

Armstrong, Clark - Range 4, Township 10 - Colored
    Laura - female, age 9   Willie - male, age 6
    Jno - male, age 8

Armstrong, F.M. - Range 9, Township 9 - White
    Ethel - female, age 13   Sulie - female, age 6
    Lewis - male, age 10

Armstrong, G.W. - Range 4, Township 10 - Colored
    Marion - male, age 9   Minnie - female, age 7

Arnold, C.H. - Pontotoc - White
    Cora - female, age 18   Lizzie - female, age 11
    Chas - male, age 17   Edna - female, age 8
    Martin - male, age 13

Arnold, W.T. - Range 4, Township 11 - White
    Cordie - female, age 10   Lula - female, age 7

Ashmore, L.A. - Range 4, Township 9 - White
    Wm - male, age 12   Jas - male, age 7
    Julia - female, age 10   Lemuel - male, age 5

Artis, Robt - Range 3, Township 20 - Colored
    Emily - female, age 15   Peter - male, age 9
    Robt - male, age 13   Lou - female, age 6

Atkins, J.T. - Range 4, Township 10 - White
    Jno - male, age 18   Ada - female, age 9
    Bessie - female, age 14   Jennie - female, age 5

Auborn, Walter - Range 4, Township 10 - White
    Etta - female, age 17   Willie - male, age 16
    Robt - male, age 18

Austin, A.H. - Range 1, Township 11 - White
    Cynthia - female, age 14   May - female, age 10
    Jno - male, age 12   Margaret - female, age 7

Austin, W.J. - Range 1, Township 11 - White
    May - female, age 17   Lucy - female, age 10
    Jas - male, age 15   W.M. - male, age 7
    Elihu - male, age 13   J.E. - male, age 5
    Sarah - female, age 13

Aycock, P.P. - Troy - White
    Modie - female, age 18   Jno - male, age 12
    Chas - male, age 17   Edna - female, age 8
    Mack - male, age 15   Ira - male, age 7
    Mattie - female, age 15   Josie - female, age 6
    Lucy - female, age 14   Vernon - male, age 5

Babb, Ben - Range 3, Township 9 - Colored
    Mat- male, age 8

Babb, T.J. - Range 3, Township 8 - White
    Sarah - female, age 17   Leslie - male, age 8
    Laura - female, age 13

Bailey, March - Range 2, Township 10 - Colored
    Bettie - female, age 15   Violet - female, age 9
    Jack - male, age 13   Sam - male, age 6
    Ida - female, age 11

Baker, A.J. - Range 3, Township 9 - White
   Tera - female, age 7   Lela - female, age 5

Baker, Chas - Range 2, Township 8 - White
   Emison - male, age 5

Baker, L.B. - Range 2, Township 8 - White
   Ida - female, age 16   Jonah - male, age 11

Baker, M.S. - Range 1, Township 9 - White
   Mattie - female, age 9

Baker, Mose - Range 4, Township 9 - Colored
   Hattie - female, age 10

Baker, W.H. - Pontotoc - White
   Chas - male, age 20   Willie - male, age 15

Baker, W.Y. - Range 2, Township 8 - White
   Isaac - male, age 14

Baldwin, S.D. - Range 4, Township 9 - White
   Lillie - female, age 11   Gilmer - male, age 7
   Louisa - female, age 9   Mart - male, age 5

Ball, A. - Range 3, Township 9 - Colored
   Leona - female, age 14   Dallas - male, age 9
   Vallie - female, age 13   Sam - male, age 7
   Rufus - male, age 12

Ball, Burrell - Range 3, Township 9 - Colored
   Andrew - male, age 18   Rona - female, age 15
   Martin - male, age 17   Jno - male, age 13

Ball, Gus - Range 3, Township 8 - Colored
   Dee - male, age 18   Mattie - female, age 12
   Fred - male, age 16   Julia - female, age 8

Ball, I.N. - Range 2, Township 10 - White
   Lula - female, age 9

Ball, Mrs. M.E. - Range 3, Township 9 - White
   Frank - male, age 18   Carry - female, age 12
   Lena - female, age 16   Jeff - male, age 10
   Geo - male, age 14   Dollie - female, age 6

Ball, Yancy - Range 3, Township 9 - Colored
   Marion - male, age 15   Thos - male, age 10
   Susie - female, age 19   Hooper - male, age 19
   Lee - male, age 9

Bandy, Jim - Range 3, Township 9 - Colored
   Anna - female, age 18   Jessee - male, age 11
   Tom - male, age 13   Sam - male, age 8

Banister, Jno - Range 3, Township 8 - White
   Etta - female, age 12

Barbee, W.C. - Toccopola - White
   Jas - male, age 13   Cleveland - male, age 6

Barksdale, H. - Range 2, Township 8 - Colored
   Larkin - male, age 14   Allie - female, age 8
   Annie - female, age 11

Barksdale, H. - Range 1, Township 9 - Colored
   Arthur - male, age 10

Barksdale, J.S. - Range 2, Township 10 - White
   Oscar - male, age 9   Robt - male, age 6

Barnett, Mrs. G. A. - Range 4, Township 11 - White
   Will - male, age 15   Robt - male, age 8
   Della - female, age 13   Pearl - female, age 5
   Jo - male, age 10

Barr, Mrs. A.E. - Range 4, Township 11 - White
   H.C. - female, age 16

Barr, S.M. - Range 3, Township 9 - White
   Minnie - female, age 15

Barksdale, W.D. - Range 2, Twonship 10 - White
   Alma - female, age 9   Eva - female, age 14
   Cortis - female, age 7   Lela - female, age 16
   Sid - male, age 5

Barefield, A.J. - Range 1, Township 11 - White
   Mattie - female, age 10

Barefield, Chas. - Range 1, Township 11 - White
   Viola - female, age 12   Emory - female, age 6
   Walter - male, age 8

Barr, Geo - Guardian - Range 3, Township 9 - Colored
   Bolton, Pearl - female, age 9   Bolton, Etta - female, age 6

Barr, Nathan - Pontotoc - Colored
   Effie - female, age 11   Wm - male, age 9
   Lizzie - female, age 10   Ann - female, age 6

Bolton, Mrs. Mallie - Range 3, Township 10 - White
   Jessee - male, age 5

Barton, Mrs. N. - Range 1, Township 11 - White
   Lela - female, age 10

Bass, J.P. - Range 4, Township 10 - White
   Robt - male, age 10   Effie - female, age 6
   Noah - male, age 8   Jas. - male, age 5

Bass, W.F. - Range 4, Township 10 - White
   Geo - male, age 10

Beard, C.C. - RAnge 2, Township 10 - White
   Walton - male, age 18   Jessie - female, age 10
   Edgar - male, age 14   Daisy - female, age 8
   Cora - female, age 12   Archie - male, age 6

Beasley, J.F. - Range 3, Township 8 - White
   Revena - female, age 19   J.W. - male, age 8
   P.A. - female, age 16   Mary - female, age 6
   Ann - female, age 14   Medona - female, age 11

Beck, Henry - Range 4, Township 10 - Colored
   Emma - female, age 18   Sam - male, age 10
   Henry - male, age 16

Beckham, Hamp - Range 3, Township 9 - Colored
   Jessee - male, age 12

Beckley, C.C. - Range 4, Township 9 - Colored
   Susie - female, age 18   Irene - female, age 13
   Eliza - female, age 16   Eddie - male, age 12
   Samantha - female, age 15   Emma - female, age 10
   Della - female, age 13   Odus - male, age 5

Beckley, E.V. - Range 4, Township 9 - Colored
   Sam - male, age 18   Minnie - female, age 6
   Patty - female, age 15   Dillard, SAm - male, age 18
   Chas - male, age 8   Dillard, Melissa - female, age 14

Beckley, H.C. - Range 4, Township 9 - Colored
   Lem - male, age 19   Estelle - female, age 9

Beckely, L.B. - Range 4, Township 9 - Colored
   Phillip - male, age 18   Siner - male, age 16

Beckley, L.E. - Range 4, Township 10 - Colored
   Sina - male, age 17   Phil - male, age 19

Beckham, Alf - Range 3, Township 9 - Colored
   Emma - female, age 6   Fannie - female, age 5

Beecham, Wm - Guardian - Range 3, Township 9 - Colored
   Owen, Mattie - female, age 11   Owen, Jno - male, age 14

Belk, H.C. - Range 1, Township 11 - White
   Julia - female, age 17   Roxie - female, age 8
   Mose - male, age 18   T.B. - male, age 19
   Ella - female, age 13

Bell, Albert - Range 3, Township 10 - Colored
   Richard - male, age 19   Wm - male, age 10
   Rachael - female, age 15   Amanda - female, age 7
   Joe - male, age 8

Bell, Albert - Range 2, Township 9 - Colored
   Judge - male, age 16   Delia - female, age 13
   Booker - male, age 14   Mary Ann - female, age 7

Bell, Andy - Pontotoc - Colored
   Walter - male, age 19   Sam - male, age 16
   Frank - male, age 17

Bell, Ike - Range 3, Township 9 - Colored
   Martha - female, age 17   Frank - male, age 7
   Lena - female, age 15   Thos - male, age 6
   Pearl - female, age 13   Ruby - female, age 5

Bell, Isaac - Range 2, Township 9 - Colored
   Exekiel - male, age 12   Jane - female, age 7
   Monroe - male, age 10

Bell, J.W. - Pontotoc - White
   Robt - male, age 13   Mary - female, age 7
   Lillian - female, age 9   Rose - female, age 15

Bell, Jim - Range 2, Township 8 - Colored
   Clarence - male, age 7   Jane - female, age 5

Bell, Mrs. M.C. - Range 4, Township 11 - White
   J.E. - male, age 14

Bell, Mrs. M.C. - Troy - White
   J.A. - male, age 18   Mollie - female, age 15

Bell, W.W. - Pontotoc - White
   Lou - female, age 18   Jno - male, age 16

Bell, S. - Range 3, Township 9 - Colored
   Lon - male, age 5   Harris, Will - male, age 13

Bell, Semella - Range 3, Township 10 - Colored
   Will - male, age 13   Lonnie - male, age 5

Bell, Will - Range 2, Township 8 - Colored
   Lena - female, age 8   Leus - female, age 5
   Reason - male, age 5

Bell, Will - Range 2, Township 8 - Colored
   Mary - female, age 6

Belyan, J.G. - Range 1, Township 9 - White
   James - male, age 7   Ada - female, age 6

Bennett, Jno - Range 4, Township 11 - Colored
   Frank - male, age 15   W.M. - male, age 8
   N.E. - male, age 13   Minnie - female, age 17
   Allie - male, age 11

Berry, Ben - Range 3, Township 8 - Colored
   Jo - male, age 7

Berry, J.H. - Range 1, Township 8 - White
   Lora - female, age 14   Nancy - female, age 7
   Jessie - female, age 12   Bonnie - female, age 5
   Mary - female, age 10

Berry, Isam - Range 4, Township 8 - Colored
   Chas - male, age 17   Ida - female, age 7
   Lewis - male, age 14   Lucy - female, age 5
   Andy - male, age 10

Berry, Mack - Range 2, Township 8 - Colored
   Linton - male, age 12   Phernezer - male, age 15
   Sherman - male, age 10   Clinton - male, age 13
   Lyss - male, age 12

Berry, N.M. - Range 3, Township 8 - White
   Jennie - female, age 18

Betts, Berry - Range 3, Township 10 - Colored
   Henry - male, age 16   Amanda - female, age 9
   Thos - male, age 16   Nelson - male, age 8
   Jas - male, age 14   Ona - female, age 5
   Ed - male, age 11

Betts, Berry - Range 3, Township 11 - Colored
   Tom - male, age 16   Amanda - female, age 8
   Henry - male, age 16   Nelson - male, age 7
   James - male, age 14   Onie - female, age 5

Betts, Chas - Range 3, Township 11 - Colored
   Armistead - male, age 12   Lewis - male, age 8

Betts, Chas - Range 3, Township 10 - Colored
   Thos - male, age 16   Ed - male, age 9
   Henry - male, age 16   Amanda - female, age 8
   James - male, age 14   Onie - female, age 5
   Armstead - male, age 12

Betts, F.M. - Range 4, Township 11 - White
   Daisy - female, age 5

Betts, J..B. - Range 4, Township 11 - White
   Arthur - male, age 5

Betts, J.B. - Range 4, Township 11 - White
   Chas - male, age 8   Jas - male, age 6

Betts, J.I. - Range 4, Township 11 - White
   Chas - male, age 8   Jas - male, age 6

Betts, Ora - Range 4, Township 11 - Colored
   Lawrence - male, age 14   Irene - female, age 8
   Vassie - female, age 10

Betts, t.H. - Range 4, Township 11 - White
   Daisy - female, age 10   Ada - female, age 6
   Lela - female, age 8

Betts, Thos - Troy - Colored
   Nannie - female, age 13   Henry - male, age 7
   Chester - male, age 11

Beckham, Willis - Range 4, Township 11 - Colored
   Elias - male, age 19   Ed - male, age 11
   Sarah - female, age 17   Martha - female, age 8
   Will - male, age 14   Mamie - female, age 6
   Leander - male, age 15

Bevel, F.W. - Range 3, Township 10 - White
   Homer - male, age 12   Maggie - female, age 5
   Luella - female, age 7

Bevell, H.P. - Range 2, Township 8 - White
   T.M. - male, age 20   Jno - male, age 9
   L.C. - male, age 17   Lonnie - male, age 7

Bevel, J.B. - Range 1, Township 10 - White
   Jas - male, age 17   Pearl - female, age 8
   Mary - female, age 13   Kate - female, age 6
   Sallie - female, age 12   Richard - male, age 5

Bevell, Marion - Range 1, Township 10 - White
   Jas - male, age 12   Bettie - female, age 8
   Lewis - male, age 11

Bevell, S.P. - Range 1, Township 10 - White
   Ben - male, age 13   Charles - male, age 8
   Geo - male, age 11   Bettie - female, age 5
   Coleman - male, age 9

Bickerstaff, M.L. - Range 3, Township 11 - White
   John - male, age 18   Wm - male, age 11
   Georgia - female, age 16   Jane - female, age 9

Bigham, D.C.M. - Range 3, Township 9 - White
   Eugene - male, age 16   Clara - female, age 8
   Virgie - female, age 13   Clinton - male, age 5
   Florence - female, age 12

Bigham, H.M. - Range 3, Township 9 - White
   Lillie - female, age 12   Jessee - male, age 7
   Willie - male, age 9   Fannie - female, age 5

Bigham, J.J. - Range 2, Township 8 - White
   Norman - male, age 5

Bigham, W.D. - Range 2, Township 8 - White
   Clinton - male, age 6

Black, Fife - Range 1, Township 10 - White
   Robt - male, age 18   Sam - male, age 14

Black, Mrs. M. - Range 2, Township 9 - White
   M.D. - male, age 19   A.C. - female, age 7

Black, Mrs. M.H. - Range 2, Township 8 - White
   Ada - female, age 14   Maudie - female, age 8
   V.H. - female, age 12   E.T. - male, age 5

Black, Roe - Range 1, Township 10 - White
   Edna - female, age 18   Mollie - female, age 11
   Josie - female, age 17   Archie - male, age 10
   Carry - female, age 15

Black, T.R. - Range 2, Township 8 - White
   B.E. - male, age 9   Dy - male, age 6
   E.Q. - male, age 8

Black, T.R. - Range 1, Township 11 - White
   Dalton - male, age 5

Blakely, G.B. - Guardian - Range 4, Township 9 - White
   Duke, Ed - male, age 20   Duke, Florence - female, age 13
   Duke, Geo - male, age 17

Blaylock, W.R. - Guardian - Range 1, Township 11 - White
   Houpt, Bettie - female, age 17

Blount, Geo - Range 3, Township 10 - Colored
   Alice - female, age 18   Clifford - male, age 10
   Eugene - male, age 15   Conard - male, age 7
   Robt - male, age 13   Rubin - male, age 5
   Frances - female, age 12

Blount, J.B. - Range 1, Township 11 - White
   Gus - male, age 19   Jim - male, age 9
   Eli - male, age 14   Levi - male, age 6
   Claud - male, age 11

Bockman, A. - Guardian - Range 1, Township 11 - White
   Barnes, James - male 18

Bockman, H. - Range 1, Township 11 - White
   Luther - male, age 6

Boland, J.L. - Range 4, Township 10 - White
   Thos - male, age 17   Chas - male, age 11
   Jas - male, age 15   Mack - male, age 7
   Wiley - male, age 13

Bolen, C.J. - Range 4, Township 9 - White
   Bulah - female, age 10   Estelle - female, age 5
   Ethel - female, age 8

Bolen, C.J. - Range 1, Township - White
   Cordie - female, age 11   Maud - female, age 7
   Claud - male, age 9

Bolen, D.N. - Range 3, Township 10 - White
   Kizzie - female, age 17   Leonard - male, age 10
   Edward - male, age 15   Minnie - female, age 8
   Austin - male, age 13

Bolen, Wm - Range 1, Township 11 - White
   Walter - male, age 18

Bolton, A.L. - Range 3, ownship 10 - Colored
   Frank - male, age 15   Mat - male, age 9
   Mary - female, age 11   Thos - male, age 8
   Nancy - female, age 13   Alf - male age 5

Bolton, Alf - Range 3, Township 10 - Colored
   Frank - male, age 15   Nannie - female, age 11
   Mary - female, age 13   Lillie - female, age 5

Bolton, C.W. - Pontotoc - White
   Frank - male, age 8   Rich'd - male, age 5
   Wm - male, age 6

Bolton, Dave - Pontotoc - Colored
   Lon - male, age 12   Jane - female, age 10

Bolton, Dick - Range 3, Township 10 - Colored
   Pauline - female, age 20   Mary - female, age 12
   Richard - male, age 16

Bolton, Sam - Range 4, Township 9 - Colored
   Susie - female, age 15   Lucy - female, age 10
   Jessie - female, age 13   Arthur - male, age 17
   Nannie - female, age 11   Sam - male, age 8
   Lucy - female, age 10

Boren, R.N. - Toccopola - White
   Sallie - female, age 19   Olgar - male, age 10
   Luella - female, age 17   Elco - male, age 8
   Marvin - male, age 14   Julia - female, age 6

Boseman, Ann - Range 3, Township 9 - Colored
   Robt - male, age 20   Lena - female, age 9
   Eb - male, age 17   Ruby - female, age 6
   Daisy - female, age 11

Bost, M.W. - Range 2, Township 8 - White
   Elvis - male, age 19   Delta - female, age 10
   Ora - female, age 17   Luther - male, age 12
   Lura - female, age 14   Donnie - female, age 6

Bost, W.W. - Range 2, Township 8 - White
   Alonzo - male, age 5

Bowman, Mrs. M.C. - Range 4, Township 9 - White
   Frank - male, age 18   Malissa - female, age 14
   Lonnie - male, age 16   Ellen - female, age 11

Box, Geo - Range 4, Township 9 - White
   Della - female, age 18   Susie - female, age 14
   Anna - female, age 16   Lydia - female, age 12

Boyd, Wm - Range 4, Township 11 - White
   Sallie - female, age 12   Simon - male, age 8
   Lon - female, age 10

Bradford, Dave - Range 3, Township 9 - Colored
   Wm - male, age 17   Mandy - female, age 13
   Pearl - female, age 15   Beatrice - female, age 10

Bradford, J.M. - Range 3, Township 8 - White
   Pearl - female, age 11   Blythe - male, age 7
   Annie - female, age 9

Bradford, Jane - Range 2, Township 9 - Colored
   Essex - male, age 5

Bradford, Judge - Pontotoc - Colored
   Fannie - female, age 16   Rich'd - male, age 12
   Poston - male, age 14

Bradford, Mary - Pontotoc - Colored
   Kate - female, age 16   Emery - male, age 12
   Irene - female, age 17   Julia - female, age 9

Bradford, P.B. - Range 3, Township 9 - Colored
   Peter - male, age 20

Bradford, Peter - Pontotoc - Colored
   Miller, Will - male, age 20

Bradford, Robt - Range 3, Township 10 - Colored
   Jennie - female, age 12   Ada - female, age 7
   Arthur - male, age 10   Lou - female, age 5

Bradford, S.R. - Range 3, Township 9 - Colored
   Howard - male, age 18   Jennie - female, age 13
   Sanford - male, age 15   Eva - female, age 11
   Maggie - female, age 16   Ona - female, age 5

Bradly, Henry - Range 4, Township 11 - Colored
   Ed - male, age 11   Morris - male, age 6
   Sam - male, age 8

Brame, A. - Range 4, Township 9 - Colored
   Adlee - female, age 14   Lovie - female, age 5

Brame, Elias - Range 4, Township 9 - Colored
   Anderson - male, age 19   Cinda - female, age 12
   Rich'd - male, age 14   Carrie - female, age 10
   Alice - female, age 16

Bramlett, J.F. - Range 2, Township 8 - White
   Hugh - male, age 12   Jennie - female, age 8
   Wm - male, age 9   Olena - female, age 6

Bramlitt, James - Range 1, Township 10 - white
   Clyde - female, age 7

Bramlett, L.M. - Range 2, Township 8 - White
   Virginia - female, age 11   Oliver - male, age 9

Bramlett, F.M. - Range 2, Township 9 - White
    Walter - male, age 10   Hubbard - male, age 6
    Zodie - female, age 7

Bramlitt, Milas - Range 4, Township 11 - Colored
    Ida - female, age 6

Bramlett, S.C. - Range 2, Township 8 - White
    Birdie - female, age 7   Jennie - female, age 5

Bramlett, T.A. - Range 3, Township 9 - White
    Erskin - male, age 17   Lawrence - male, age 11
    Clemmie - female, age 16   Thos - male, age 9
    Edgar - male, age 14   Annie - female, age 6
    Jessee - male, age 12   Floried - female, age 5

Brandon, C.F. - Range 4, Township 9 - White
    Dock - male, age 20   Ben - male, age 14
    Thos - male, age 18   Will - male, age 12
    Robt - male, age 16   Ausbon - male, age 7

Brandon, Jas - Range 4, Township 9 - White
    Jas - male, age 13   Lucy - female, age 8
    Oscar - male, age 10   Morris - male, age 5
    Mary - female, age 11

Brandon, Lee - Range 4, Township 9 - Colored
    Love - male, age 6

Brandon, T.D. - Range 2, Township 8 - White
    Willie - male, age 10   Denson - male, age 8
    Daisy - female, age 11   Lilian - female, age 6
    Lela - female, age 9

Bratton, J.L. - Range 1, Township 10 - White
    Jodie - female, age 16   Joe - male, age 11

Bray, C.S. - Range 2, Township 11 - White
    Lizzie - female, age 19   Sam - male, age 13
    May - female, age 17   Ben - male, age 11
    John - male, age 15   Henry - male, age 9
    Chas - male, age 13   Mattie - female, age 8
                                            Rosa - female, age 7

Brazile, J.W. - Range 4, Township 11 - White
    J.W. - male, age 15   F.M. - female, age 6
    L.J. - female, age 13

Brazile, P.B. - Range 4, Township 9 - White
    Mamie - female, age 9   Adline - female, age 11

Brewer, Mrs. - Range 4, Township 10 - White
    Cy - male, age 8   Elizabeth - female, age 7

Brewster, Jo - Range 3, Township 8 - Colored
    Will - male, age 10   Ella - female, age 8

Briggs, M.A. - Range 1, Township 11 - White
    Ella - female, age 12   Lucy - female, age 6

Bright, J.C. - Pontotoc - White
    Alice - female, age 5

Britts, J.S. - Range 2, Township 11 - White
   O.L. - female, age 12   Mattie - female, age 18

Britts, Sam - Range 1, Township 11 - White
   Jane - female, age 15   Jno - male, age 6
   Sallie - female, age 8

Brooks, L.R. - Range 3, Township 10 - White
   Jeanette - female, age 18   Emma - female, age 13
   Lizzie - female, age 15   Idella - female, age 6

Brooks, Neal - Pontotoc - Colored
   Wm - male, age 8   Lewis - male, age 5
   Fowler - male, age 10

Broom, R.F. - Range 2, Township 10 - White
   Lela - female, age 13   Alma - female, age 7
   Lusher - male, age 11   Robt - male, age 5
   Bessie - female, age 9

Brown, A.F. - Range 4, Township 9 - White
   Wm - male, age 9   Lewis - male, age 7

Brown, Abe - Range 3, Township 11 - Colored
   Ed - male, age 13   Hynie - female, age 6

Brown, B. - Range 2, Township 11 - White
   Tucker - male, age 18

Brown, C.A. - Range 4, Township 9 - White
   Eddie - male, age 6   Willie - male, age 5

Brown, D.H. - Range 1, Township 11 - White
   Wm - male, age 8   Hattie - female, age 5

Brown, H.H. - Range 1, Township 11 - White
   Laura - female, age 10

Brown, J.O. - Range 4, Township 9 - White
   Allen - male, age 17   Lewis - male, age 10
   Mattie - female, age 15   Bosewell - male, age 8
   Rena - female, age 12   Robt - male, age 6

Brown, Jeff D. - Pontotoc - White
   H. - male, age 9

Brown, Mrs. S.A. - Range 1, Township 11 - White
   Wm - male, age 9   Lucy - female, age 10

Brown, R.P. - Pontotoc - White
   Minnie - female, age 16   Georgia - female, age 10
   Lula - female, age 12   Ruby - female, age 6

Brown, W.L. - Range 3, Township 9 - White
   Mary - female, age 5

Brown, W.R. - Guardian - Range 4, Township 9 - White
   Waldo, Pearl - female, age 7   Waldo, Chester - male, age 5
   Waldo, Cora - female, age 6

Browning, J.E.A. - Range 3, Township 8 - White
   Annie - female, age 6   Effie - female, age 5

Broyles, Taylor - Range 2, Township 10 - Colored
   Nettie - female, age 9   Dorsey - male, age 7

Bruce, W.R. - Range 4, Township 8 - White
   Wm - male, age 18   Albert - male age 13
   Robt - male, age 16

Bryant, G.T. - Range 4, Township 9 - White
   Colie - female, age 9   Sallie - female, age 5
   Jno - male, age 8

Bryant, H.B. - Range 4, Township 11 - White
   Permelia - female, age 19   Wm - male, age 12
   Anna - female, age 15   Robt - male, age 6
   Bessie - female, age 10

Bryant, Mack - Range 4, Township 11 - White
   Mary - female, age 16   Bessie - female, age 10
   Eva - female, age 14   Luther - male, age 9
   Rufus - male, age 12   Jno - male, age 8

Bryant, Sarah - Range 4, Township 10 - White
   Henry - male, age 18   Jno - male, age 13
   Ora - female, age 15

Bryant, T.F. - Range 2, Township 10 - White
   Jas - male, age 18

Buchanan, Ann - Pontotoc - Colored
   Robt - male, age 12   Lucy - female, age 9

Buchanan, W.M. - Troy - White
   Jack - male, age 18   Oliver - male, age 13
   Cleland - male, age 17   Orvelle - female, age 10
   Clyde - female, age 15

Buchanan, J.E. - Range 1, Township 11 - White
   Mary Jane - female, age 15   Josiah - male, age 6

Buchanan, J.M. - Range 3, Township 11 - White
   Curt- male, age 10   Jessie - male, age 13
   Robt - male, age 15   Lee - male, age 19

Buchanan, J.M. - Range 3, Township 11 - White
   Curtis - male, age 20   Josie - female, age 15
   J.G. - male, age 17   Luna - female, age 12

Buchanan, Mrs. M.A. - Range 4, Township 11 - White
   Jas - male, age 19   Nolan, Ida - female, age 11
   Nolan, Savannah - female, age 16   Nolan, Fannie - female, age 9
   Nolan, Lela - female, age 14

Buchanan, S.D. - Range 4, Township 9 - White
   Flora - female, age 18   Ida - female, age 12
   Carry - female, age 16   Florence - female, age 10
   Elvira - female, age 14   Alice - female, age 8

Buchanan, Young - Range 2, Township 8 - Colored
   Ida - female, age 14   Yancy - male, age 7
   Jeff - male, age 10   Cornelia - female, age6
   Alf - male, age 8

Buchanan, J.D.B. - Range 2, Township 8 - White
   H.A. - male, age 9　　　　　　　　　　M.E. - female, age 5
   C.C. - female, age 7

Buchanan, S.P. - Range 2, Township 8 - White
   Bud - male, age 18　　　　　　　　　　Jno - male, age 14

Bullard, Henry - Range 2, Township 8 - White
   Fannie - female, age 16　　　　　　　　Lillie - female, age 14

Burke, Mrs. E.E. - Range 3, Township 11 - White
   Rich'd - male, age 15

Burks, J.H. - Range 2, Township 8 - White
   Ira - female, age 5

Burlison, J.R. - Range 4, Township 11 - White
   Jas - male, age 16　　　　　　　　　　Wm - male, age 9
   Lula - female, age 14　　　　　　　　　Henry - male, age 7
   Meddie - female, age 12　　　　　　　　Effie - female, age 5

Burson, R.A. - Range 1, Township 11 - White
   Pearl - female, age 16　　　　　　　　　Bertha - female, age 6
   Lena - female, age 14

Butler, G.R. - Range 4, Township 9 - White
   Estelle - female, age 12　　　　　　　　Frank - male, age 7
   Ernest - male, age 10

Butler, Mrs. R.S. - Range 4, Township 10 - White
   Martha - female, age 17　　　　　　　　Thos - male, age 15

Caffey, Jeff - Range 4, Township 11 - Colored
   Lee - male, age 9　　　　　　　　　　　Peter - male, age 7

Cain, Virgil - Range 4, Township 9 - Colored
   Charity - female, age 11　　　　　　　　Jeff - male, age 7
   Arthur - male, age 8　　　　　　　　　　Jettie - female, age 6

Calamise, Andrew - Range 4, Township 9 - Colored
   Aaron - male, age 19　　　　　　　　　Mary - female, age 16

Caldwell, B.W. - Range 3, Township 9 - White
   Mary - female, age 16　　　　　　　　　Julius - male, age 10
   Artemas - female, age 14　　　　　　　　Lewis - male, age 5
   Purnia - female, age 12

Caldwell, I.H. - Range 3, Township 9 - White
   Tera - female, age 19　　　　　　　　　Jessie - female, age 12
   Ulton - male, age 17　　　　　　　　　　Roy - male, age 5
   Pearl, female, age 14

Caldwell, J.A. - Range 2, Township 10 - White
   Lula - female, age 14　　　　　　　　　Ethel - female, age 6
   Artie - female, age 11　　　　　　　　　James - male, age 7

Caldwell, J.C. - Range 4, Township 9 - White
   Press - male, age 6　　　　　　　　　　Chas - male, age 13
   Emma - female, age 11

Caldwell, J.L. - Range 3, Township 9 - White
   Walter - male, age 13   Lin - male, age 7
   Luther - male, age 8   Etta - female, age 11

Caldwell, J.R. - Range 3, Township 9 - White
   Montie - female, age 10   Ester - male, age 7

Caldwell, J.W., Sr. - Range 4, Township 9 - White
   Ebbie - male, age 19   Beval - male, age 12

Caldwell, James - Range 2, Towsnhip 11 - White
   Ella - female, age 13

Caldwell, Jas - Range 1, Township 11 - White
   Lillie - female, age 8   Julia - female, age 6

Caldwell, Jas - Range 1, Township 9 - White
   W.T. - male, age 17   Lou - female, age 20

Caldwell, James - Range 1, Township 9 - Colored
   Lonnie - male, age 6   Lou - female, age 20
   W.T. - male, age 17

Caldwell, J.C. - Range 2, Township 11 - White
   Eula - female, age 12

Caldwell, Mrs. F.N. - Range 4, Township 9 - White
   Walter - male, age 19   Cora - female, age 12
   Press - male, age 14   Mamie - female, age 10
   Delia - female, age 16

Caldwell, S.W.D. - Range 4, Township 9 - White
   Minnie - female, age 17   Mary - female, age 12
   Edna - female, age 15   Pressly - male, age 8
   Willie - male, age 13   Pearl - female, age 6

Caldwell, W.Y. - Range 4, Township 8 - White
   Willie - female, age 17   Thos - male, age 15

Calhoun, J.A. - Range 2, Township 9 - Colored
   Annie - female, age 6   Wm - male, age 5

Calloway, J.J. - Range 3, Township 11 - White
   Thos - male, age 18   Lou - female, age 7
   Frank - male, age 13   Jennie - female, age 5

Calloway, W.F. - Range 4, Township 10 - White
   Onie - female, age 5

Cameron, Calvin - Range 3, Township 11 - Colored
   Hosea - male, age 18   Neshra - male, age 14
   Walton - male, age 13   Ezekiel - male, age 7
   Lem - male, age 10   Professor - male, age 5

Cameron, Jack - Range 3, Township 11 - Colored
   Rosetta - female, age 18   Stella - female, age 9
   Cy - male, age 16   Corena - female, age 7
   Judge - male, age 15   Clement - female, age 5
   Edgar - male, age 11

Cammeron, A. - Range 3, Township 11 - White
   Cora - female, age 17   Lizzie - female, age 10
   Mary - female, age 14   Thos - male, age 6
   Joe - male, age 12   Emma - female, age 5

Campbell, B.R. - Range 3, Township 9 - White
   Cora - female, age 12　　　　　　　　Vara - female, age 10

Campbell, J.W. - Range 4, Township 11 - White
   Chas - male, age 18　　　　　　　　　Rubin - male, age 12
   Thos - male, age 17　　　　　　　　　Robt - male, age 10
   Wm - male, age 15　　　　　　　　　　Emma - female, age 6

Campbell, W.C. - Range 4, Township 10 - White
   Jas - male, age 19　　　　　　　　　　Alma - female, age 16

Campbell, W.R. - Guardian - Range 3, Township 9 - White
   Homan, Jno - male, age 16

Cannon, Jack - Range 2, Township 11 - Colored
   Robt - male, age 19　　　　　　　　　Lizzie - female, age 12
   Sam - male, age 17　　　　　　　　　　Estelle - female, age 10
   J.D. - male, age 15　　　　　　　　　Clinton - male, age 8

Capewell, Wm - Range 4, Township 11 - White
   Ida - age 16

Carnes, Mrs. Ella - Range 2, Township 10 - White
   Jennie - female, age 19　　　　　　　Sallie - female, age 15
   Susie - female, age 17

Carnes, T.R. - Range 2, Township 8 - White
   R.O. - male, age 19　　　　　　　　　Ovella - female, age 6
   Emma - female, age 8　　　　　　　　Elmer - male, age 5

Carpenter, J.W. - Range 1, Township 10 - White
   Tibitha - female, age 17　　　　　　Jennie - female, age 8
   Jno - male, age 13　　　　　　　　　　Wm - male, age 6
   Zora - female, age 11

Carpenter, Jas - Range 4, Township 10 - White
   Gabe - male, age 6

Carr, F.A. - Pontotoc - White
   Robt - male, age 8

Carr, H.P. - Range 1, Township 11 - White
   Mack - male, age 11　　　　　　　　　Mattie - female, age 7

Carr, Ike - Range 1, Township 11 - White
   Mattie - female, age 12　　　　　　　Julia - female, age 16
   Rich'd - male, age 10

Carr, J.T. - Range 1, Township 10 - White
   Wm - male, age 19　　　　　　　　　　Jas - male, age 10
   Paraduse - female, age 13　　　　　　Ollie - female, age 5

Carr, J.W. - Range 1, Township 11 - White
   Ophelia - female, age 6

Carr, N. - Range 1, Township 11 - White
   Susie - female, age 8

Carr, O.C. - Pontotoc - White
   Lawrence - male, age 16　　　　　　　Erskin - male, age 10
   Lottie - female, age 14　　　　　　　Isaac - male, age 6
   Frank - male, age 12

Carruth, L.O. - Range 4, Township 9 - White
   Lora - female, age 6

Carter, A. - Range 2, Township 10 - White
   Henderson - male, age 20   John - male, age 14
   Dora - female, age 18   Jack - male, age 12

Carter, B.D. - Range 1, Township 8 - White
   Edgar - male, age 15   Lula - female, age 8
   Elvina - female, age 13   Loyce - female, age 5
   Haton - male, age 11

Carter, Cal - Range 4, Township 10 - Colored
   Thos - male, age 15   Fannie - female, age 6
   Joe - male, age 12

Carter, G.W. - Range 3, Township 9 - White
   Clarence - male, age 8   Belle - female, age 7

Carter, J.M. - Pontotoc - White
   J.M. - male, age 19   G.R. - male, age 16
   J.W. - male, age 17   E. - male, age 14
   H.H. - female, age 15

Carter, Mrs. James - Range 1, Township 8 - White
   Eula - female, age 16   James - male, age 8
   Oliver - male, age 10   Mack - male, age 6

Carvin, Ralph - Range 3, Township 10 - Colored
   Jennie - female, age 16   Mattie - female, age 12
   Rosa - female, age 15   Lawyer - male, age 6
   Mary - female, age 14   Andrew - male, age 5
   Frances - female, age 9

Carwyle, Geo - Range 2, Township 8 - White
   Della - female, age 6

Carwyle, Mrs. S.A. - Range 2, Township 8 - White
   Frank - male, age 12

Carwyle, W.S. - Range 2, Township 8 - White
   Jno - male, age 8   Dora - female, age 5

Cason, Adam - Range 4, Township 10 - Colored
   Geo - male, age 11

Castleberry, Mrs. A.B. - Pontotoc - White
   Lawrence - male, age 19   Chas - male, age 13
   Robt - male, age 15

Castleberry, S. - Range 3, Township 11 - Colored
   Vance - male age 16   Cora - female, age 12
   Ann - female, age 14   Lula - female, age 9

Castleberry, Sandy - Range 3, Township 10 - Colored
   Vance - male, age 6   Minnie - female, age 9
   Anna - female, age 14   Lou - female, age 6
   Cora - female, age 12

Castleberry, Wm - Range 4, Township 11 - White
   Nancy - female, age 13   Virginia - female, age 7
   Sarah - female, age 10   Lela - female, age 5

Cates, J.M. - Range 2, Township 9 - White
- Mary - female, age 20
- Augustus - male, age 18
- Mattie - female, age 15
- Rose - female, age 13
- Geo - male, age 11
- Alice - female, age 9
- Fannie - female, age 7
- Mittie - female, age 5

Cates, Peter - Range 4, Township 10 - Colored
- Callie - female, age 11
- Annie - female, age 8
- Ed - male, age 5

Chenault, J.H. - Range 3, Township 11 - White
- Ruthy - female, age 16
- Ludie - female, age 14
- Agnes - female, age 11
- Ida - female, age 8

Cherry, Jim - Range 4, Township 10 - Colored
- Jim - male, age 16

Chestine, D.J. - Range 1, Township 9 - White
- Susie - female, age 5

Chew, F. - Range 3, Township 9 - Colored
- Hill - male, age 18
- Annil - female, age 16
- Fleet - male, age 15
- Mattie - female, age 13
- Ben - male, age 11
- Effie - female, age 6
- Lena - female, age 5

Childrell, L.M. - Range 2, Township 8 - White
- Emma - female, age 12
- Anna - female, age 10
- Marvis - male, age 6

Chisolm, Adam - Range 2, Township 8 - Colored
- Mary - female, age 18
- Hannah - female, age 15

Chisolm, F.H. - Pontotoc - Colored
- Proctor - male, age 20

Chisolm, I.J. - Range 4, Township 11 - White
- Ila - female, age 5

Clark, A.J. - Pontotoc - White
- M.R. - male, age 20
- Ruby - female, age 12

Clay, Mrs. M.C. - Range 2, Township 9 - White
- Edgar - male, age 15
- Jessee - male, age 13
- Lena - female, age 9
- Mary - female, age 8
- Jno - male, age 6

Clayton, Mrs. S.C. - Range 3, Township 9 - White
- Joe - male, age 20
- Mat - male, age 18

Clayton, W.N. - Range 3, Township 9 - White
- Augie - female, age 13
- Maggie - female, age 1
- Robt - male, age 8
- Sallie - female, age 6

Clement, M.N. - Range 4, Township 11 - White
- Sarah - female, age 20
- Sam - male, age 17
- Onie - female, age 11
- Nettie - female, age 11

Clements, A.S. - Range 1, Township 10 - White
- Chas - male, age 13
- Lettie - female, age 10

Clements, D.F. - Range 1, Township 10 - White
- Lee - male, age 13
- Jas - male, age 11
- Lena - female, age 5

Clements, J.H. - Range 1, Township 10 - White
    Alice - female, age 12
    Posey - male, age 10
    Willie - male, age 8
    Carl - male, age 6
    Mary - female, age 5

Coates, A.A. - Range 1, Township 10 - White
    Fannie - female, age 18
    Henry - male, age 15
    Willie - male, age 13
    Chas - male, age 8
    Mattie - female, age 11
    Daisy - female, age 7
    Doney - female, age 5

Cobb, H.C. - Range 2, Township 8 - White
    Anna - female, age 15
    G.E. - male, age 14
    E.L. - male, age 10

Cobb, H.L. - Range 2, Township 8 - White
    Lizzie - female, age 14
    Clara - female, age 10
    Lula - female, age 8
    Lillie - female, age 5

Cobb, James - Range 4, Township 8 - Colored
    Willie - male, age 12
    Della - female, age 12
    Thos - male, age 14
    Susie - female, age 10

Cobb, Lewis - Range 2, Township 8 - Colored
    Oscar - male, age 12
    Jno - male, age 8

Cobb, Marcus - Range 2, Township 8 - Colored
    Annie - female, age 16
    Joe - male, age 5

Cole, G.C. - Range 1, Township 11 - White
    Cora - female, age 16
    Lester - male, age 10
    Rubin - male, age 8
    Willie - male, age 5

Cole, Geo., Sr. - Range 3, Township 9 - Colored
    Frank - male, age 13
    Lena - female, age 9
    Walter - male, age 6

Cole, H.C. - Range 2, Township 8 - Colored
    Charlotte - female, age 13
    Fannie - female, age 11
    Pearl - male, age 10
    Oscar - male, age 8

Cole, J.B. - Range 1, Township 11 - White
    Barney - male, age 12
    Laudie - male, age 8

Coleman, Isam - Range 2, Township 10 - Colored
    Mary - female, age 14
    Rose - female, age 15
    Mollie - female, age 12
    Isam - male, age 10
    Minor - male, age 8
    John - male, age 6

Coleman, W.H. - Range 3, Township 11 - White
    Emily - female, age 7
    Lewis - male, age 15
    Willie - male, age 14
    Holley - male, age 13
    Jas - male, age 12

Coleman, J.H.C. - Range 2, Township 8 - White
    Lee - male, age 16
    Henry - male, age 12
    Ada - female, age 7
    Madia - female, age 5

Collins, Dave - Range 4, Township - Colored
    Adline - female, age 18
    Jno - male, age 15

Collins, J.H. - Range 3, Township 11 - White
   Arthur - male, age 18   Ollie - male, age 7
   Sam - male, age 14   Vernor - male, age 5
   Hardy - male, age 9

Collums, D.B. - Range 1, Township 10 - White
   Maud - female, age 11   Rosa - female, age 5
   Carry - female, age 7

Collums, D.B. - Guardian - Range 1, Township 10 - White
   Douglas, Thos - male, age 20

Collums, J.P. - Range 1, Township 10 - White
   Andra - male, age 20   Ethel - female, age 8
   Asker - male, age 10

Collums, Monroe - Range 1, Township 10 - White
   Floyd - male, age 18

Conlee, C.W. - Range 2, Township 8 - White
   Lee - male, age 17   Oscar - male, age 11
   Carry - female, age 15   Rosco - male, age 9
   Walter - male, age 13   Jessee - male, age 7

Conlee, E.C. - Range 2, Township 8 - White
   Jennie - female, age 18   Luvenia - female, age 12
   Bell - female, age 17   Lyman - male, age 14
   Jno - male, age 16   Clarence - male, age 8

Conlee, Wm - Range 2, Township 8 - White
   T.P. - male, age 18   E.E. - male, age 9
   C.E. - male, age 15   C.H. - male, age 5
   L.F. - male, age 13

Cook, Geo - Range 2, Township 10 - Colored
   Jas - male, age 18   Georgia - female, age 10
   Jano - male, age 16   Ben - male, age 8
   Ada - female, age 14   Arthur - male, age 6
   Bettie - female, age 12

Cook, J.R. - Range 3, Township 11 - White
   Helen - female, age 10   James - male, age 6
   Revella - female, age 8   Ladelle - female, age 5

Cook, R. - Range 2, Township 9 - White
   C.H. - female, age 19   M.E. - female, age 12
   C.S. - female, age 17   J.L. - male, age 10

Cooper, Alice - Range 3, Township 11 - Colored
   Hubbard - male, age 9   Ida - male, age 5
   Ada - female, age 5

Cooper, J.B. - Range 3, Township 11 - White
   Wm - male, age 16   Sam - male, age 14

Cooper, T.J. - Guardian - Range 2, Township 8 - White
   Sadler, Henry - male, age 12

Cord, Mrs. B.T. - Range 1, Township 11 - White
   Joe - male, age 14

Corder, L. - Range 2, Township 8 - White
   Minnie - female, age 13   Chas - male, age 7
   Jas - male, age 11   Claud - male, age 5
   Maudie - female, age 8

Cornelius, Aaron - Range 2, Township 8 - White
   Albert - male, age 18   Jodie - female, age 12
   Chas - male, age 16   Anna - female, age 9
   Grace - female, age 14   Bell - female, age 6

Couch, Dock - Range 3, Township 8 - Colored
   Oliver - female, age 8   Ivy - male, age 7

Couch, W.C. - Range 3, Township 8 - White
   Jas - male, age 10   Alice - female, age 7
   Ira - male, age 8

Cowsert, T.H. - Range 1, Township 11 - White
   Mary - female, age 12   Jno - male, age 8
   Jas - male, age 10   Harriett - female, age 6

Cox, Enoch - Pontotoc - White
   Sudie - female, age 9   Estella - female, age 7

Cox, J.C. - Range 2, Township 8 - White
   Estella - female, age 14   Carry - female, age 7
   Willie - male, age 12   Arthur - male, age 6

Cox, J.M. - Range 2, Township 11 - White
   Maud - female, age 14

Craig, J.M. - Range 1, Township 11 - White
   Tom - male, age 20   Jas - male, age 9
   Lucy - female, age 13   Estelle - female, age 6

Craig, M.S. - Range 3, Township 9 - White
   Joe - male, age 12   Joe - male, age 9
   Robt - male, age 12   Marion - male, age 8
   Chester - male, age 9   Eva - female, age 15
   Claud - male, age 10

Crane, M.L. - Range 4, Township 9 - White
   Carrie - female, age 20   Walker, Thos - male, age 17

Crawford, Frank - Range 3, Township 10 - Colored
   Pink - male, age 10   Jane - female, age 6
   Lula - female, age 8   Robt - male, age 5

Crawford, Joe - Range 3, Township 9 - Colored
   Manda - female, age 17   Robt - male, age 8
   Annie - female, age 15   Henry - male, age 5

Crawford, Sarah - Pontotoc - Colored
   Mary - female, age 12

Crawford, T.J. - Range 3, Township 11 - White
   Pearl - male, age 12   Evin - male, age 8
   Dwight - male age 10

Crawford, W.C., Jr. - Range 2, Township 10 - White
   Sulie - female, age 17   Thos - male, age 9
   Nannie - female, age 15   Hester - female, age 5
   Jno - male, age 12

CRawford, W.C., Sr. - Range 2, Township 10 - White
   GEo - male age 15   Lena - female, age 11

Crawford, W.H. - Range 3, Township 11 - White
   Wm - male, age 16

Crawford, W.H.D. - Range 3, Township 11 - White
   Sam - male, age 19   Giles - male, age 15
   Leta - female, age 17   Hattie - female, age 9
   Claud - male, age 13   Willie - male, age 7

Creed, J.C. - Range 3, Township 10 - White
   Willie - male, age 6

Creed, P.T. - Range 3, Township 11 - White
   Minnie - female, age 18   Ida - female, age 11
   Mary - female, age 15   Rich'd - male, age 13

Crensaw, Mose - Range 3, Township 9 - Colored
   Jas - male, age 9   Jno - male, age 8

Crocker, Ann - Range 2, Township 11 - Colored
   E.S. - male, age 18   A.J. - male, age 12
   Mattie - female, age 16   Henry - male, age 9
   F. - male, age 14

Crocker, Ann - Range 3, Township 8 - Colored
   Josie - female, age 12   Henry - male, age 7
   Jno - male, age 10

Crocker, J.D. - Range 4, Township 11 - White
   Lame - male, age 12

Crocker, Jim - Range 3, Township 8 - Colored
   Carry - female, age 14   Clarence - female, age 8
   Sam - male, age 10   Geo - male, age 6

Crosby, W.D. - Range 3, Township 9 - White
   Clara - female, age 9   Walter - male, age 6
   Cornelia - female, age 8   Estella - female, age 5
   Fred - male, age 7

Crow, Mrs. - Range 4, Township 11 - White
   Gus - male, age 20   Jeff - male, age 12
   Bill - male, age 17   Ira - female, age 10
   Jas - male, age 15

Cunningham, Turner - Range 4, Township 10 - Colored
   Harvy - male, age 10   Douglas - male, age 5

Cruse, Henry - Range 3, Township 10 - White
   Florence - female, age 11

Cruse, H.A. - Range 3, Township 9 - White
   Annie - female, age 10   Modenia - female, age 6

Cruse, J.M. - Range 3, Township 10 - White
   Jno - male, age 10   Jennie - female, age 7

Cruse, J.T. - Range 3, Township 10 - White
   Willie - male, age 17   Walter - male, age 15
   Callie - female, age 18   Alma - female, age 12

Cummings, J.B. - Range 1, Township 9 - White
   Buford - male, age 17   Henry - male, age 11
   Curt - male, age 15   Pinkie - female, age 8
   Handly - male, age 13

Cummings, L. - Range 1, Township 10 - White
   M.B. - male, age 12

Daggett, C.W. - Range 4, Township 10 - White
   E.L. - male, age 10   Annie - female, age 5

Daggett, Sam - Range 4, Township 11 - Colored
   Morrison - male, age 14   Joanah - male, age 7
   Lula - female, age 10

Dandridge, Henry - Range 3, Township 9 - Colored
   Josie - female, age 17   Robt - male, age 14
   Bettie - female, age 16   Garfield - male, age 9

Dandridge, Horace - Range 3, Township 10 - Colored
   Sarah - female, age 16   Sylvester - male, age 7
   Will - male, age 14

Daniel, J.C. - Range 1, Township 11 - White
   Maud - female, age 5

Daniel, Mr.s. S.B. - Range 1, Township 11 - White
   Isom - male, age 20   Allen - male, age 15
   Jennie - female, age 19   Allie - male, age 14
   Ann - female, age 15

Darling, C.P. - Range 4, Township 8 - White
   Minnie - female, age 10   Lonnie - male, age 6
   Alice - female, age 8

Daueer, Jo - Troy - Colored
   Sarah - female, age 19   Jas - male, age 6

Davenport, J.M. - Pontotoc - White
   Paul - male, age 6

Davis, A.B. - Range 3, Township 11 - White
   Birtie - female, age 19   Lizzie - female, age 16

Davis, Ab - Range 2, Township 11 - White
   Britton - male, age 19   John - male, age 16

Davis, Adline - Range 4, Township 10 - Colored
   Albert - male, age 19   Robt - male, age 10
   Walter - male, age 12

Davis, Allen - Range 1, Township 10 - White
   Levi - male, age 8   Drucella - female, age 10

Davis, Amos - Range 1, Township 10 - White
   J.T. - male, age 13   Silas - male, age 5
   Minnie - female, age 6   R.M. - male, age 20

Davis, G.A. - Range 4, Township 9 - White
   Walter - male, age 15   Cora - female, age 10
   Gaines - male, age 13   Lou - female, age 7
   Lawton - male, age 11

Davis, G.P. - Range 1, Township 10 - White
   Delma - male, age 12   Virginia - female, age 5

Davis, J.G. - Toccopola - White
   Alvin - male, age 11   Jessee - male, age 4
   Alma - female, age 11   Hattie - female, age 6

Davies, J.D. - Range 4, Township 11 - Colored
   Joe - male, age 15   Estelle - female, age 9
   Effie - female, age 14   Eva - female, age 6
   Lou - female, age 12

Davis, Lem - Range 4, Township 9 - Colored
   Mary - female, age 19

Davis, R.K. - Range 4, Township 11 - White
   Newt - male, age 19   Rufus - male, age 10
   Jasper - male, age 17   Savena - female, age 8
   Bee - male, age 14   Staten, Robt - male, age 18
   Geo - male, age 12

Davis, T.C. - Range 4, Township 11 - White
   Geo - male, age 15   Carroll - male, age 8
   Henry - male, age 11   Lena - female, age 6

Davis, W.A. - Range 4, Township 10 - White
   Euzella - female, age 10   Baker, Chas - male, age 20
   May - female, age 8   Baker, Will - male, age 15
   Bud - male, age 5

Dea, J.W. - Range 3, Township 9 - White
   Annie - female, age 10   Elna - female, age 6
   Sam - male, age 8

Dearman, G.I. - Range 4, Township 9 - White
   Littleton - male, age 16   Dan'l - male, age 8
   Wm - male, age 14   Leona - female, age 6

Deaton, J.F. - Range 1, Township 10 - White
   Jno - male, age 17   Lillie - female, age 10
   Dona - female, age 15   Wid - male, age 8
   Flora - female, age 13   Carry - female, age 6

DeJarnett, C.P. - Pontotoc - White
   Ellen - female, age 20   Alice - female, age 14
   Emma - female, age 17

DeJarnett, J.E. - Pontotoc - White
   Lou - female, age 13   Jno - male, age 7

Dennis, Wallace - Range 2, Township 9 - Colored
   Will - male, age 12   Bonnie - female, age 8
   Fannie - female, age 10

Dent, J. - Range 2, Township 11 - Colored
   Elvira - female, age 16   Jennie - female, age 10
   Isaac - male, age 13

Dent, Jessee - Range 4, Township 10 - Colored
   Emanuel - male, age 14   Nathan - male, age 6
   Jno - male, age 13

Dewell, A.P. - Range 4, Township 9 - White
   Willie - male, age 18   Felix - male, age 8
   Miller - male, age 14   Rosco - male, age 6
   Lee - male, age 10

Dews, Walter - Range 2, Township 10 - White
   Pearl - female, age 10   Jessie - female, age 7

Dickson, Mrs. F.S. - Range 2, Township 8 - White
   Zunie - female, age 5

Dickson, W.B. - Range 2, Township 8 - White
   Wm - male, age 15

Dickson, W.B. - Range 2, Township 9 - White
   C.C. - male, age 20   Mollie - female, age 20

Dillard, A.R. - Range 1, Township 8 - White
   Eva - female, age 8   Monie - female, age 5

Dillard, Chas - Range 4, Township 10 - Colored
   Chas - male, age 13   Robt - male, age 8
   Jno - male, age 9   Rena - female, age 6

Dillard, Dave - Range 4, Township 9 - Colored
   Vina - female, age 12   Irene - female, age 9
   Cenix - female, age 11

Dillard, E.L. - Range 1, Township 8 - White
   Albert - male, age 19   Joe - male, age 5
   Nora - female, age 13   Frances - female, age 7

Dillard, G.D. - Range 3, Township 9 - White
   Nannie - female, age 15   Jno - male, age 9
   Joshua - male, age 13   Robt - male, age 6
   Willie - male, age 12

Dillard, J.W. - Range 4, Township 8 - White
   Berry - male, age 19   Ida - female, age 17

Dillard, Jeff - Range 4, Township 9 - Colored
   Sam - male, age 16   Clara - female, age 8
   Press - male, age 10

Dillard, Joe - Range 2, Township 8 - White
   J.P. - male, age 19   Addie - female, age 16

Dillard, L.E. - Range 1, Township 10 - White
   Virginia - female, age 17   H.P. - male, age 5
   N.B. - male, age 14

Dillard, J.P. - Range 1, Township 8 - White
   Burton - male, age 19   Lura - female, age 10
   Linnie - female, age 14   Nannie - female, age 5

Dillard, P.A. - Range 3, Township 9 - White
   Mannie - male, age 12   Willie - male, age 6
   Mary - female, age 10

Dillard, J.T. - Range 1, Township 8 - White
   Earnest - male, age 12   Bettie - female, age 7
   Ivy - male, age 10

Dillard, R.D. - Range 3, Township 9 - White
   Jno - male, age 16   Annie - female, age 14
   Ed - male, age 12   Minnie - female, age 6

Dillard, T.B. - Range 4, Township 8 - White
   Cora - female, age 9   Lonnie - male, age 5
   Samuel - male, age 7

Dillard, W.H. - Range 3, Township 9 - White
   Lizzie - female, age 7

Dillard, W.B. - Range 1, Township 9 - White
   C.C. - male, age 20   Mollie - female, age 20

Dixon, Sam - Range 1, Township 10 - Colored
   Willis - male, age 9   Nannie - female, age 5
   Rose - female, age 13

Dixon, Sam - Range 1, Township 9 - Colored
   Rosa - female, age 13   Nannie - female, age 5
   Willis - male, age 9

Dodd, J.A. - Range 1, Township 9 - White
   Wiley - male, age 13   John - male, age 7
   Chester - male, age 11   Jack - male, age 5
   Lula - female, age 10

Dogan, Bush - Range 4, Township 11 - Colored
   Emma - female, age 17   Teater - male, age 9
   Kate - female, age 15

Dogan, Nancy - Range 4, Township 10 - Colored
   Chas - male, age 7   Annie - female, age 6

Donaldson, F. - Range 3, Township 10 - Colored
   Mary - female, age 12

Donaldson, J.J. - Pontotoc - White
   Souter, Clara - female, age 8

Donaldson, J.P. - Range 3, Township 10 - White
   Robt - male, age 11   Sallie - female, age 8

Donaldson, R.H. - Range 3, Township 10 - White
   Walter - male, age 18   Willie - male, age 5
   Mattie - female, age 8

Donaldson, T.A. - Range 3, Township 10 - White
   Robt - male, age 15   Henry - male, age 10
   Egbert - male, age 12   Katie - female, age 5

Donaldson, W. - Range 3, Township 10 - White
   Wm - male, age 18   Leslie - male, age 12

Donaldson, W.E. - Range 3, Township 10 - White
   Jas - male, age 16   Alice - female, age 5
   Henry - male, age 8

Doss, Foster - Range 2, Township 10 - Colored
   Sarah - female, 19   Jennie - female, age 9
   Allen - male, age 14   Mary - female, age 5
   Carry - female, age 12

Doss, George - Range 1, Township 9 - Colored
   Bud - male, age 11   Jane - female, age 18
   Henry - male, age 7

Doss, John - Range 3, Township 11 - Colored
   James - male, age 11   Dock - male, age 7
   Lum - male, age 9

Douglas - J.M. - Range 1, Township 10 - White
   Jennie - female, age 16   Medora - female, age 10
   Belzora - female, age 14   Lula - female, age 8
   Roselle - female, age 12   Joe - male, age 6

Douglas, Lou - Guardian - Range 1, Township 11 - White
   Griffen, Lee - male, age 19   Douglas - female, age 17
   Griffen, Cora - female, age 18

Douglas, S.J. - Range 1, Township 10 - White
   Alvin - male, age 16   Lula - female, age 10
   Lillie - female, age 12   Ester - male, age 6

Douglas, S.J. - Range 1, Township 11 - White
   Alvin - male, age 16   Lou - female, age 10
   Lydia - female, age 12   Estelle - female, age 6

Douglas, J.M. - Guardian - Range 1, Township 10 - White
   Durham, Jack - male, age 20   Durham, Susie - female, age 19

Dowell, P.A. - Range 4, Township 10 - White
   H.W. - male, age 19   L.E. - female, age 10
   N.J. - male, age 15   J.R. - male, age 8
   F.G. - male, age 11

Dover, T.J. - Range 1, Township 11 - White
   Cordelia - female, age 19   Joe - male, age 7

Dowdy, J.H. - Range 2, Township 8 - White
   Wm - male, age 9   Robt - male, age 5

Dozier, Jno - Range 4, Township 9 - Colored
   Jim - male, age 6

Dozier - Range 4, Township 9 - White
   Annie - female, age 20

Duke, James - Range 3, Township 10 - Colored
   Willie - male, age 8   Daisy - female, age 6

Duke, Jas - Range 3, Township 11 - Colored
   Willie - male, age 8   Daisy - female, age 6

Duke, Martin - Range 3, Township 11 - Colored
   Sallie - female, age 18   Robt - male, age 11
   Sam - male, age 16   Martin - male, age 9
   Hattie - female, age 14   Julia - female, age 8
   Savannah - Female, age 13   Ida - female, age 6

Duke, R.V. - Range 3, Township 11 - White
   M. - female, age 10   Davis - male, age 8
   Wm - male, age 9   Rich'd - male, age 5

Duke, Sam - Range 3, Township 10 - Colored
   Sam - male, age 15   Jim - male, age 12
   John - male, age 16

Duke, W.J. - Range 3, Township 11 - White
   Vada - female, age 6

Duke, Wm - Range 3, Township 10 - Colored
   Clarence - male, age 10   Lizzie - female, age 6
   Sam - male, age 7

Duncan, J.F. - RAnge 2, Township 8 - White
   I.O. - male, age 17   R.E. - male, age 8
   G.J. - male, age 14   R.D. - male, age 6
   A.B. - male, age 12

Duncan, J.S. - Range 2, Township 8 - White
   Ed - male, age 18   Effie - female, age 20

Duken, Chas - Range 4, Township 11 - Colored
   Jno - male, age 10   Han - male, age 5
   Butler - male, age 7

Dunevant, F. - Pontotoc - White
   Duff, Boon - male, age 11   Dunevant, Maud - female, age 6
   Duff, Albert - male, age 8

Dupree, Spencer - Range 2, Township 10 - White
   Ella - female, age 7   Cora - female, age 5

Eads, Burrell - Range 4, Township 9 - Colored
   Rosa - female, age 11   Archie - male, age 6
   Zedrick - male, age 7

Echols, Ab - Range 1, Township 10 - White
   Maggie - female, age 7

Echols, John - Range 2, Township 9 - White
   M. - male, age 11   H.Y. - female, age 9

Eddington, B.F. - Range 3, Township 11 - White
   Mollie - female, age 18   Mallie - female, age 11
   Sidney - male, age 16   Anna - female, age 8
   Etta - female, age 13

Eddington, E.H. - Range 4, Township 11 - White
   Elias - male, age 8   Grover - male, age 5

Edwards, Alf - Range 4, Township 9 - Colored
   Tallie - female, age 20   Hannah - female, age 12
   Chas - male, age 17   Missouri - female, age 6
   Wes - male, age 14

Edwards, Wes - Range 3, Township 10 - Colored
   Josie - female, age 10   Duke, Bettie - female, age 15
   Geo - male, age 8   Duke, Lizzie - female, age 11
   Lou - female, age 5   Duke, Oscar - male, age 14
   Duke, Bettie - female, age 15   Duke, Jas - male, age 7
   Duke, Alf - male, age 5

Edwards, Jas - Range 2, Township 10 - White
   Willie - male, age 19   Jas - male, age 10
   Vidie - female, age 17   Wm - male, age 8
   Mira - female, age 15

Edwards, W.A. - Range 2, Township 10 - White
   Robt - male, age 18   Clarence - male, age 10
   E. - male, age 16   Lou - female, age 5
   Fletcher - male, age 14

Edwards, W.B. - Range 4, Township 11 - White
   Meddie - female, age 16   Lee - male, age 12

Ellis, J.U. - Range 3, Township 11 - White
   Edgar - male, age 19   Geo - male, age 12

Ellis, Adline - Range 4, Township 11 - Colored
   Elbert - male, age 15   Lewis - male, age 8
   Pauline - female, age 11

Ellis, W.H. - Range 3, Township 11 - White
   Minnie - female, age 20   Willie - male, age 16
   Birdie - female, age 18

Ellison, J.F. - Range 3, Township 9 - White
   Sallie - female, age 12   Lewis - male, age 8
   Joe - male, age 10   Josie - female, age 6

Elzy, Amos - Range 4, Township 11 - Colored
   Clark - male, age 16   Frank - male, age 10
   Mollie - female, age 18   Allie - male, age 8
   Hadley - male, age 14

Elzy - Chas - Range 3, Township 10 - Colored
   Chas - male, age 5

Eubank, C.D. - Range 4, Township 10 - White
   Agnes - female, age 20   Meddie - male, age 10
   Lillie - female, age 19   Era - female, age 8
   Lucius - male, age 15   Lizzie - female, age 5
   Rome - male, age 13

Eubanks, W.B. - Range 4, Township 11 - White
   Jas - male, age 18   Anna - female, age 14
   Arthur - male, age 16   Cordelia - female, age 7
   F.L. - male, age 11   Birdie - female, age 6
   P.M. - male, age 10

Eudell, Chas - Range 3, Township 11 - Colored
   Aggie - female, age 16   Al - female, age 12
   Dave - male, age 14   Ruthy - female, age 8

Evans, E.M. - Range 2, Township 11 - White
   Albert - male, age 6

Evans, J.L. - Range 1, Township 11 - White
   Mattie - female, age 5

Evans, Jake - Range 2, Township 11 - Colored
   Aggie - female, age 18   Dave - male, age 14

Fair, W.T. - Range 1, Township 10 - White
   Leroy - male, age 14   Lena - female, age 6
   Ollie - female, age 10

Farrar, Dennis - Range 2, Township 9 - Colored
    Susie - female, age 16   Lennie - female, age 7
    Lizzie - female, age 13   Dolph - male, age 5

Farrar, J.T. - Range 2, Township 8 - White
    Levertie - female, age 6

Farrar, W.C. - Range 2, Township 8 - White
    Susie - female, age 17   Nora - female, age 13
    Marion - male, age 15

Faulkner, Mrs. S.S. - Troy - White
    Claudie - male, age 16   Meddie - female, age 10
    Carlton - male, age 15   Dollie - female, age 8
    Jessie - female, age 11   Elva - male, age 6

Faulkner, A.S. - Range 4, Township 9 - White
    Carmelia - female, age 10   Everett - male, age 7
    Willie - male, age 9   Wiley - male, age 5

Faulkner, F.G. - Range 4, Township 9 - White
    Anna - female, age 13   Eddie - male, age 9
    Lena - female, age 11   Geo - male, age 5

Faulkner, J.T. - Range 4, Township 9 - White
    Calvin - male, age 18   Byron - male, age 9
    Sam - male, age 14   Oscar - male, age 6
    Cora - female, age 12

Ferguson, B.F. - Range 1, Township 11 - White
    Lawrence - male, age 13   Nancy - female, age 9
    Lee - male, age 11   Minnie - female, age 5

Ferguson, E.M. - Range 1, Township 10 - White
    Sim - male, age 13   Cora - female, age 8
    Paul - female, age 10

Ferguson, E.M. - Guardian - Range 1, Township 10 - White
    McGuirt, Jno - male, age 17

Ferguson, R.S. - Range 2, Township 10 - White
    Edgar - male, age 7   Sadie - female, age 5

Ferguson, W.H. - Range 3, Township 9 - White
    Elbert - male, age 5

Ferguson, W.F. - Range 1, Township 10 - White
    Kittie - female, age 18

Field, J.A. - Range 3, Township 9 - White
    Geo - male, age 19   Jno - male, age 11
    David - male, age 17   Sarah - female, age 9
    Mary - female, age 16   Julia - female, age 7
    Gory - female, age 14   Lydia - female, age 5

Field, W.M. - Guardian - Range 3, Township 9 - White
    Cruse, Ludie - female, age 6

Fields, J.F. - Range 3, Township 10 - White
    Robt - male, age 8   Jessee - male, age 6

Fitzpatrick, Mack - Range 3, ownship 11 - Colored
    Wilson - male, age 14   Venus - male, age 9

Fitzpatrick, Nelson - Range 3, Township 11 - Colored
   Rice - male, age 18   Dink - male, age 14
   Bluford - male, age 16   Richard - male, age 8

Flaherty, F.L. - Range 3, Township 11 - White
   Lena - female, age 10   Jas - male, age 8

Flaherty, H.A. - Range 4, Township 11 - White
   Magasr. - male, age 8   Jessie - female, age 6

Flaherty, M. - Range 4, Towsnhip 9 - White
   Effie - female, age 17   Lula - female age 10
   Anna - female, age 16   Maud - female, age 6
   Pearsall - female, age 13

Flaherty, M.E. - Range 2, Township 11 - White
   Rosa - female, age 17   Alma - female, age 12
   Valdora - female, age 15   Lena - female, age 8

Flaherty, M.E. - Range 2, Township 11 - White
   Rose - female, age 17   Lena - female, age 8
   Waldro - male, age 15   Nettie - female, age 5
   Alma - female, age 12

Fleming, Peter - Range 3, Township 10 - Colored
   Peggy - female, age 16   Nellie - female, age 13
   Sallie - female, age 13   Andrew - male, age 7

Fleming, W.C. - Range 3, Township 11 - White
   Joe - male, age 15   Baily - male, age 9
   Lucious - male, age 13   George - male, age 7
   Nancy - female, age 12

Fleming, W.J. - Range 4, Township 9 - White
   Maggie - female, age 14   Lee - male, age 11
   Cora - female, age 13   Wallace - male, age 7

Fleming, W.S. - Range 4, Township 11 - White
   Jas - male, age 20   Mary - female, age 7
   Wiley - male, age 9

Fletcher - G.G. - Range 4, Township 9 - Colored
   Geo - male, age 16   Hunter - male, age 8
   Gar - male, age 13   Lapoelon - male, age 5
   Harriett - female, age 11

Floyd, F. - Range 3, Township 10 - Colored
   Savannah - female, age 7

Floyd, Geo - Range 4, Township 9 - Colored
   Ophelia - female, age 16   Henry - male, age 14

Floyd, Price - Range 4, Township 10 - Colored
   Jettia - female, age 5   Leslie, Josh - age 19

Fontaine, B.B. - Pontotoc - White
   P.H. - male, age 14   Celia - female, age 11
   G.C. - female, age 12   P.D. - male, age 7
   M.C.A. - male, age 8   B.B. - male, age 5

Fontaine, C.D. - Pontotoc - White
   Hugh - male, age 15   Helen - female, age 10
   Bessie - female, age 14   Emma - female, age 8
   Sam - male, age 12

Fontaine, Dave - Pontotoc - Colored
   Dave - male, age 15
   Jas - male, age 10
   Jno - male, age 9
   Ed - male, age 16
   Frank - male, age 12

Fontaine, J.D. - Pontotoc - White
   Chas - male, age 18
   Andrew - male, age 16
   Mary - female, age 12
   J.B. - male, age 20

Fontaine, Jas - Range 3, Township 9 - Colored
   Sarah - female, age 16
   Clara - female, age 14
   Jas - male, age 12
   Lottie - female, age 9

Fontaine, Julia - Pontotoc - Colored
   Maggie - female, age 7
   Lou - female, age 5

Fontaine, Mrs. B.G. - Pontotoc - White
   Pattie - female, age 18

Fontaine, N. - Range 2, Township 10 - White
   Paul - male, age 12
   Cora - female, age 10
   Mary - female, age 7

Fooshee, E.M. - Range 1, Township 10 - White
   Parlee - female, age 13
   Lula - female, age 11
   Ollie - female, age 7
   Della - female, age 5

Fooshee, J.R. - Range 1, Township 10 - White
   Nancy - female, age 16

Ford, Alf - Range 4, Township 11 - Colored
   Emma - female, age 18
   Fayette - male, age 17
   Geo - male, age 15
   Addie - female, age 11
   Ethel - female, age 9
   Jane - female, age 7

Ford, Kate - Range 4, Township 10 - Colored
   B.W. - male, age 20
   Etta - female, age 18
   Jodie - female, age 18

Ford, Kittie - Range 4, Township 10 - Colored
   Brewster - male, age 18
   Ella - female, age 16
   Julia - female, age 6

Foster, J.R. - Range 4, Township 11 - White
   Wm - male, age 16
   Walter - male, age 13
   Susie - female, age 11
   Lillie - female, age 7

Foster, Jane - Range 4, Township 10 - Colored
   Robt - male, age 15
   Jas - male, age 13

Fowler, D.W. - Range 4, Township 11 - White
   H.H. - male, age 16
   C.M. - male, age 12
   C.W. - male age 10

Fowler, Miles - Troy - White
   Cannon, Georgia - female, age 12

Fowler, Mrs. A. - Range 4, Township 11 - White
   Modenia - female, age 14

Foy, Jno - Range 4, Township 9 - White
   Gub - male, age 13
   Thos - male, age 9
   Ester - male, age 7

Francis, Henry - Range 4, Township 11 - Colored
   Sam - male, age 13   Aggie - female, age 11

Franklin, B.E. - Range 2, Township 10 - White
   Oscar - male, age 17   Donnie - male, age 12
   Lonnie - male, age 14   Georgia - female, age 7

Franklin, Geo - Range 4, Township 9 - Colored
   Henderson - male, age 18   Modena - female, age 9
   Thos - male, age 20   Georgia - female, age 8
   Ezell - male, age 16   Ozie - female, age 5
   Callie - female, age 12

Franklin, J.B. - Range 2, Township 10 - White
   Oscar - male, age 16   Culis - female, age 8
   Mollie - female, age 13   Tishey - female, age 5
   Lee - male, age 12

Franklin, J.C. - Range 1, Township 11 - White
   Florence - female, age 10   Maud - female, age 6
   Geo - male, age 9

Franklin, Mollie - Range 4, Township 9 - Colored
   Willie - male, age 16   Irish - male, age 10

Franklin, Wesly - Range 4, Township 9 - Colored
   Arthur - male, age 17   Hybernia - male, age 9
   Clarence - male, age 16   Wesly - male, age 6
   Lawrence - male, age 12

Frazier, J.A. - Range 1, Township 9 - White
   Etta - female, age 18   James - male, age 13
   Joe - male, age 16   Susie - female, age 7

Frazier, W.H. - Range 1, Township 9 - White
   Richard - male, age 18   Margaret - female, age 11
   John - male, age 16   Adline - female, age 9

Freeman, Easter - Range 1, Township 11 - Colored
   Bettie - female, age 11   Oscar - male, age 5

Freeman, Hannah - Range 1, Township 11 - Colored
   Eliza - female, age 19   Alex - male, age 9
   Albert - male, age 11

Freeman, Nathan - Range 4, Township - Colored
   Birdie - female, age 6   Lonnie - male, age 13
   Estelle - female, age 15

Freeman, S.M. - Range 1, Township 11 - White
   Lela - female, age 12   Walter - male, age 6
   Clifford - male, age 10   Judson - male, age 5
   Claud - male, age 8

Freeman, T.H. - Range 1, Township 11 - White
   Lewis - male, age 16   Phillip - male, age 7
   Clyde - female, age 12   Ben - male, age 5
   Fannie - male, age 7

Fretwell, Mrs. - Range 3, Township 9 - White
   Will - male, age 14   Mattie - female, age 8

Frierson, Eli - Range 4, Township 10 - Colored
   Fred - male, age 15   Fayette - male, age 6
   Della - female, age 10   Holman - male, age 5

Frierson, W.V. - Pontotoc - White
   Jno - male, age 16   Evander - male, age 11
   Vincent - male, age 13

Fuqua, A.F. - Range 4, Township 11 - White
   L.E. - male, age 19   A.G. - male, age 15
   W.E. - male, age 17   A.M. - female, age 13

Fuqua, C.W. - Range 4, Township 10 - White
   Wm - male, age 17   Maggie - female, age 12
   Sam - male, age 15

Fuqua, W.P. - Range 4, Township 10 - White
   Lavinder - male, 11   Effie - female, age 5
   Lena - female, age 9

Furr, W.M. - Toccopola - White
   Nora - female, age 20   Marvie - male, age 11
   Celma - female, age 17   Rich'd - male, age 6
   May - female, age 14   Myrtle - female, age 12
   Estelle - female, age 9

Gaines, Dick - Range 4, Township 9 - White
   Jno - male, age 14   Joanna - female, age 8

Gaines, M.H. - Range 2, Township 9 - White
   Frank - male, age 10

Gaines, R.W. - Range 4, Township 9 - White
   Mattie - female, age 11   Mormon, Lillie - female, age 15
   Willie - male, age 9

Gaines, W.H. - Range 2, Township 9 - White
   Frank - male, age 10   Julia - female, age 5

Golding, Shields - Range 1, Township 9 - Colored
   Mat - female, age 2-   Bessie - female, age 8
   Tobe - female, age 18   Cornelia - female, age 9
   Lou - female, age 14   Nettie - female, age 6
   Nancy - female, age 12

Galloway, D.W. - Range 1, Township 11 - White
   Maggie - female, age 16   Ludy - female, age 8
   Minnie - female, age 10

Galloway, Geo - Range 2, Township 11 - White
   E.B. - male, age 19   Mattie - female, age 18

Gambrell, W.S. - Guardian - Range 4, Township 8 - White
   Griffin, Chas - male, age 13   Griffin, Minnie - female, age 15
   Griffin, Claudie - female, age 12

Gardner, E.O. - Range 2, Township 8 - White
   Irene - female, age 17   Festus - male, age 14
   Lee - male, age 15   Lula - female, age 11

Gardner, Henry - Range 3, Township 11 - Colored
   Tilden - male, age 16   Warren, male, age 8
   Anna - female, age 13   George - male age 5

Gardner, M.T. - Troy - White
   H.B. - male, age 19   Dan - male, age 11
   Wm - male, age 17   Lewis - male, age 8
   Hanson - male, age 15   M.W. - male, age 6
   Kittie - female, age 13

Garmon, Ella - Range 4, Township 10 - Colored
    Georgia - female, age 10   Wm - male, age 6

Garmon, Mrs. M.E. - Troy - White
    Cora - female, age 12   Ollie - female, age 7
    Odus - male, age 9   Lillie - female, age 5

Garrett, E.W. - Range 4, Township 10 - Colored
    Will - male, age 18   E.M. - female, age 14
    Frank - male, age 16   Elvira - female, age 12
    I.E. - female, age 16   Thos - male, age 8

Garrett, John - Range 3, Township 11 - Colored
    Steven - male, age 20   Ellen - female, age 13
    Fontaine - male, age 17   Ola - female, age 10
    Willie - male, age 16   John - male, age 5
    Ida - female, age 15

Garrison, Mrs. M.A. - Range 2, Township 10 - White
    Anna - female, age 15   Estelle - female, age 12

Garrison, T.B. - Range 2, Township 10 - White
    Martha - female, age 19   Mollie - female, age 11
    Lou - female, age 16   Lewis - male, age 9
    Jessee - male, age 13   Rena - female, age 6

Gates, J.W. - Range 3, Township 8 - White
    Bettie - female, age 17

Gates, S.S. - Range 2, Township 9 - White
    Lela - female, age 16   Kate - female, age 5

Gay, Mrs. S.M. - Range 4, Township 11 - White
    Freeman - male, age 19

Geeter, W.J. - Range 1, Township 9 - White
    Anna - female, age 8   Claud - male, age 7

Geeter, W.J. - Range 4, Township 10 - White
    A.M. - female, age 11   W.W. - male, age 9

Gentry, J.N. - Range 1, Township 11 - White
    Lee - male, age 16

Gentry, J.T. - Range 3, Township 10 - White
    Jno - male, age 15   Gip - male, age 7
    Mary - female, age 13   Tilda - female, age 5
    Andy - male, age 10

George, S.L. - Range 2, Township 10 - White
    Tucker - male, age 11   Jas - male, age 6

Gideon, Mrs. Sarah - Troy - White
    Milton - male, age 18   Belle - female, age 14

Gilbert, A.T. - Range 4, Township 11 - White
    Obedie - male, age 18   Martin - male, age 10
    Thos - male, age 16   Edna - female, age 8
    Chas - male, age 14   Robt - male, age 15
    Sam - male, age 12

Gilder, R.B. - Range 2, Township 8 - White
    Era - female, age 5

Gilder, R.H. - Range 2, Township 8 - White
   Wm - male, age 14   Dalton - male, age 8
   Carry - female, age 10   Lora - female, age 6

Gillespie, J.D. - Range 2, Township 10 - White
   Lillie - female, age 7

Gillespie, T.J. - Range 1, Township 11 - White
   Annie - female, age 20   Hartley - male, age 9
   Willie - male, age 18   Marzie - female, age 6
   Lon - male, age 14   Lum - male, age 5
   Dovie - female, age 12

Gilmer, A. - Range 4, Township 10 - Colored
   Callie - male, age 14   Pearl - female, age 15

Gilmer, J.M. - Range 2, Township 10 - White
   Cordie - female, age 8   Maud - female, age 5
   Carr - male, age 7

Gilmer, W.B. - Toccopola - White
   J.S. - male, age 19   J.T. - male, age 7
   E.L. - male, age 11

Givhan, Ardy - Range 4, Township 10 - White
   Mariah - female, age 17   Will - male, age 12
   Babe - female, age 13   Josie - female, age 8

Givhan, Dave - Range 4, Township 10 - Colored
   Jno - male, age 14   Geo - male, age 10

Givhan, Jno - Range 4, Township 10 - Colored
   Love - male, age 10   Babe - male, age 7

Givhan, Joe - Range 4, Township 11 - Colored
   Julia - female, age 10   Jno - male, age 5
   Ezekiel - male, age 10

Givhan, Lewis - Range 4, Township 10 - Colored
   Evaline - female, age 10   Burrell - male, age 7
   Julia - femle, age 11   B.M. - male, age 5

Givhan, Moses - Range 4, Township 11 - Colored
   Mose - male, age 20   Enly - male, age 15
   Jake - male, age 17   Thos - male, age 12
   Paul - male, age 16   Misses - female, age 6

Glover, Wesly - Range 3, Township 9 - Colored
   Ida - female, age 12   Clarence - female, age 6
   Pinkney - male, age 10

Godfrey, J.E. - Range 1, Township 11 - White
   R.D. - male, age 18   H.M. - male, age 14

Godfrey, W.H. - Range 4, Township 10 - White
   Sallie - female, age 10   Wm - male, age 7

Goggans, J.T. - Range 2, Township 9 - White
   Minnie - female, age 6

Goggans, Jack - Range 4, Township 9 - White
   Anna - female, age 20   Dock - male, age 16
   Elihu - male, age 19

Goggans, S. - Range 2, Township 9 - White
    Ed - male, age 6

Goggans, W.H. - Range 2, Township 9 - White
    Martha - female, age 16   Millie - female, age 12
    Tilden - male, age 14

Golden, Geo - Range 3, Township 8 - Colored
    Ona - female, age 16   Edna - female, age 9

Golden, H.J. - Range 2, Township 9 - White
    Jno - male, age 17

Golden, Harry - Range 2, Township 9 - Colored
    Annie - female, age 20   Maggie - female, age 13
    Mattie - female, age 18   Etta - female, age 15
    Carroll - female, age 17   Florence - female, age 7
    Minnie - female, age 15   J.W. - male, age 5

Golden, Shield - Range 2, Township 9 - Colored
    Mat - female, age 20   Vaney - female, age 12
    Tode - female, age 18   Bessie - female, age 8
    Lou - female, age 14   Cornelia - female, age 9

Golding, Geo - Range 1, Township 9 - Colored
    Atta - female, age 5   Ad - male, age 12

Goldman, W.M. - Range 3, Township 10 - White
    Hubbard - male, age 7

Gooch, C. - Range 1, Township 10 - White
    Lou - female, age 15   Newt - male, age 9
    Tingsly - female, age 13   Modena - female, age 5
    Dee - male, age 11

Gooch, W.A. - Range 2, Township 9 - White
    Lee - male, age 8   S.A. - female, age 5
    Annie - female, age 6

Goode, Mrs. N.B. - Guardian - Range 3, Township 10 - White
    Barton, Robert - male, 7

Goodlett, G.A. - Range 4, Township 9 - White
    Lafayette - male, age 11   Lillie - female, age 8

Goodwin, J.E. - Range 1, Township 11 - White
    Myrtle - female, age 5

Goodwin, J.E. - Range 1, Township 11 - White
    Onie - female, age 17   Eva - female, age 10
    Coley - female, age 15   Maud - female, age 8
    Colley - female, age 12   Cora - female, age 6

Goodwin, J.P. - Range 4, Township 11 - White
    Azby - male, age 8   Arthur - male, age 5
    Carry - female, age 7

Goodwin, J.T. - Range 4, Township 11 - White
    Chas - male, age 8   Josie - female, age 5
    Mark - male, age 7

Gordon, J. - Range 3, Township 10 - Colored
    Rebecca - female, age 10   Henry - male, age 9

Gordon, Jas - Range 3, Township 10 - White
   Robt - male, age 16

Gordon, M.C. - Range 3, Township 10 - Colored
   Annie - female, age 12   Mamie - female, age 6
   Allie - female, age 10   Jas - male, age 5
   Susie - female, age 8

Gordon, Wm - Range 3, Township 10 - Colored
   Callie - female, age 18   Hattie - female, age 13
   Julia - female, age 15   Mary - female, age 5

Grace, N.J. - Range 1, Township 10 - White
   Cora - female, age 11

Grady, W.A. - Range 3, Township 9 - White
   Ida - female, age 15   Rubin - male, age 10
   Bedelle - female, age 14   Annie - female, age 8

Graham, L.D. - Range 3, Township 8 - White
   Marcus - male, age 6

Graham, S.A. - Guardian - Range 1, Township 8 - hite
   Hardin, B. - gemale, age 10   Todd, Julia - female, age 11
   Todd, Ben - male, age 8   Todd, Abe - male, age 16

Graham, Mrs. S.D. - Range 1, Township 8 - White
   Joe - male, age 18   James - male, age 12
   John - male, age 14   Rufus - male, age 9

Grant, G.A. - Range 4, Township 10 - White
   Estelle - female, age 19   Vallie - female, age 12
   Mattie - female, age 17   Edgar - male, age 5

Grant, L.D. - Pontotoc - Colored
   Josie - female, age 18   Birdie - female, age 12
   Walter - male, age 16   Sanford - male, age 16
   Rich'd - male, age 14

Gray, A.G. - Range 4, Township 9 - White
   Jno - male, age 19

Gray, J.D. - Range 4, Township - White
   Clifford - male, age 9

Gray, J.H. - Range 1, Township 11 - White
   Jennie - female, age 10   Armedia - female, age 5
   Artie - female, age 9   Aaron - male, age 18
   Anna - female, age 5

Gray, Jack - Range 3, Township 9 - Colored
   Geo - male, age 15   Henry - male, age 13

Gray, Will - Range 3, Township 10 - Colored
   Robt - male, age 11   Verna - female, age 8
   Lou - female, age 10   Walter - male, age 5

Green, Geo - Range 3, Township 9 - Colored
   Annie - female, age 19

Green, T.J. - Range 1, Township 9 - White
   Walter - male, age 14   Jessie - female, age 8
   Willie - female, age 18   Mattie - female, age 6

Gregory, Ann - Range 4, Township 11 - Colored
    Mary - female, age 15   Sam - male, age 10
    Calvin - male, age 14   Geo - male, age 8
    Wallace - male, age 12   Maud - female, age 6

Gregory, E.G. - Range 1, Township 10 - White
    Jno - male, age 18   Salena - female, age 12
    Willie - male, age 15

Gregory, J.B. - Range 3, Township 10 - White
    Mattie - female, age 14   Andrew - male, age 10

Gregory, J.E. - Range 1, Township 9 - White
    Thos - male, age 11   Green - male, age 6

Gregory, S.J. - Range 2, Township 10 - White
    Annie - female, age 17   Jennie - female, age 13
    Eddie - male, age 15   Fannie - female, age 8

Gregory, Smug - Range 3, Township 11 - Colored
    Boalam - male, age 20

Gregory, W.R. - Range 1, Township 10 - White
    Jno - male, age 20   Dock - male, age 12
    Alice - female, age 18   Mattie - female, age 10
    Sallie - female, age 16   Coleman - male, age 8
    Ida - female, age 14   Eddie - male, age 5

Griffin, Jessee - Range 1, Township 11 - White
    Mattie - female, age 18   Maud - female, age 12
    Virgie - female, age 16   Porter - male, age 5

Grissom, A.A. - Range 2, Township 8 - White
    lela - female, age 10   Annie - female, age 6
    Isaac - male, age 8

Grissom, J.W. - Range 2, Township 8 - White
    Lige - male, age 16   Wm - male, age 10
    Walter - male, age 15   Mattie - female, age 9
    Joe - male, age 12   Mary - female, age 8

Grisson, Mrs. M.J. - Range 2, Township 8 - White
    Lonnie - male, age 12   Lydia - female, age 8
    Carmelia - female, age 10

Guthrey, R.G. - Range 2, Towsnhip 8 - White
    Virginia - female, age 5

Guinn, W.W. - Range 3, Township 9 - White
    Willie - male, age 5

Gunn, A.J. - Range 1, Township 9 - White
    Geo - male, age 13   Nancy - female, age 9
    Sam - male, age 11   Sue - female, age 6

Gunter, Lewis - Range 4, Township 11 - Colored
    Lewis - male, age 17   Chas - male, age 6
    Anna - female, age 15   Thos - male, age 5
    Emma - female, age 18   Mary - female, age 19

Hadley, Thos - Range 4, Township 11 - White
   Oscar - male, age 17

Hal, Jane - Range 2, Township 9 - Colored
   Susie - female, age 8

Hall, A.H. - Range 4, Township 9 - White
   Hudson - male, age 16

Hall, Harvy - Range 3, Township 10 - Colored
   Pinson, Mose - male, age 20   Lee - male, age 13
   Jim - male, age 17   Frank - male, age 10
   Howard - male, age 15

Halsell, R.M. - Range 3, Township 11 - White
   Annie - female, age 6

Hamilton, J.M. - Range 1, Township 10 - White
   Roxie - female, age 15   Sallie - female, age 12

Hamilton, Jno - Range 1, Township 10 - White
   Wash - male, age 10   Zammer - female, age 8

Hancock, Jeff - Range 3, Township 10 - Colored
   L.A. - male, age 20   Hattie - female, age 8
   Nora - female, age 16   Eliza - female, age 7
   Mat - male, age 13   Wm - male, age 8

Hancock, Jeff - Range 3, Township 11 - Colored
   Silas - male, age 20   Lizzie - female, age 16

Hancock, Mrs. L.E. - Range 2, Township 10 - White
   Willie - male, age 17   Fannie - female, age 13
   Tom - male, age 15   Callie - female, age 11

Haney, J.B. - Range 2, Twonship 8 - White
   Willie - male, age 18   Anna - female, age 14

Haney, J.F. - Range 4, Township 10 - White
   Hattie - female, age 7

Haney, I.T. - Range 4, Township 11 - White
   Ennis - male, age 17   Lewis - male, age 12
   Joe - male, age 14

Haney, R.L. - Range 3, Township 10 - White
   Curtis - male, age 5

Haney, S.C. - Range 1, Township 11 - White
   Hattie - female, age 16   Sam - male, age 8
   Bettie - female, age 13

Haney, S.M. - Range 3, Township 10 - White
   E.M. - male, age 13   M.D. - female, age 9

Harden, D.M. - Range 4, Township 10 - White
   Chas - male, age 15   Sam - male, age 8
   Eliza - female, age 13   Annie - female, age 5
   Jno - male, age 11

Hardin, A.C. - Range 3, Township 10 - White
   Lou - female, age 9   Ennice - male, age 7

Hardin, A.F. - Guardian - Range 3, Township 9 - White
   Burton, Robt - male, age 11

Hardin, Jim - Range 3, Township 8 - Colored
   Lula - female, age 19

Hardin, Orange - Range 3, Township 8 - Colored
   Lee - male, age 6   Jim - male, age 12

Hardin, Robt - Range 4, Township 10 - Colored
   Oliver - male, age 15   Lydia - female, age 10
   Lenard - male, age 13   Mallie - female, age 8

Hardin, W.T. - Range 3, Township 9 - White
   Ju - male, age 17   Hastaline - femle, age 10

Hardin, W.Y. - Range 3, Township 9 - Colored
   Lizzie - female, age 6

Hardy, Joe - Toccopola - White
   Eva - female, age 20

Hare, Mrs. Lizzie - Range 1, Township 11 - White
   Addie - female, age 5   Susie - female, age 10
   Robt - male, age 12   Margaret - female, age 7

Harkness, G.R. - Range 4, Township 11 - White
   Alonzo - male, age 9   Jno - male, age 5
   Baxter - male, age 7

Harlow, W.W. - Range 4, Township 10 - White
   Will - male, age 20   Effie - female, age 13
   Chas - male, age 18   Lit - male, age 12
   Sam - male, age 16   Thad - male, age 9

Harmon, J.A. - Range 4, Township 11 - White
   Jessee - male, age 12   Wm - male, age 8
   Arthur - male, age 10

Harmon, J.S. - Range 4, Township 11 - White
   Willie - male, age 20   Pink - mlae, age 11
   Jno - male, age 17   Vester - male, age 8
   Fannie - female, age 14   Anna - female, age 5

Harper, Bolen - Range 4, Township 9 - Colored
   Essie - female, age 7   Andy - male, age 16

Harper, Chas - Range 4, Township 8 - Colored
   John - male, age 19   Dave - male, age 17

Harper, J.G. - Range 4, Township 8 - Colored
   Minnie - female, age 7   Henry - male, age 5

Harper, Range 2, Township 9 - Colored
   Ed - male, age 13   Whit - male, age 7
   Mary - female, age 10   John - male, age 5
   Caroline - female, age 9

Harrill, Lena - Pontotoc - Colored
   Maggie - female, age 13   Malinda - female, age 5
   Lou - female, age 11

Harris, Frank - Range 4, Township 9 - Colored
   Froney - female, age 12   Wilson, Clifton - male, age 16
   Dillard, Sam - male, age 16   Hamilton, Lawrence - male, age 9

Harris, H.H. - Range 3, Township 11 - White
   Daisy - female, age 20   Freeman - male, age 9
   Woodbry - male, age 14   Ceil - male, age 7
   Aaron - male, age 12

Harris, J.W. - Range 1, Township 11 - White
   Walter - male, age 10   Leslie - male, age 7

Harris, J.W. - Range 2, Township 10 - White
   Ethel - female, age 9   Quitton - male, age 6

Harris, L.F. - Range 3, Township 11 - White
   Annie - female, age 17   Arthur - male, age 9
   Mattie - female, age 16   Qbelle - female, age 8
   Buford - male, age 14   Sallie - female, age 7
   Leacy - male, age 12

Harris, Sandy - Range 3, Township 10 - Colored
   Nora - female, age 12   Frank - male, age 9
   Mattie - female, age 11   Sam - male, age 6

Harris, T.M. - Range 2, Township 8 - White
   Herman - male, age 8   Eula - female, age 6

Harrison, L.E. - Guardian - Range 1, Township 10 - hite
   Rogers, Sarah - female, age 6

Hartley, Mrs. M.J. - Range 4, Township 22 - White
   Marion - male, age 19   Ed - male, age 14
   Albert - male, age 17   Anna - female, age 11
   Berry - male, age 14   Lewis - male, age 8

Hartley, Z.T. - Range 4, Township 11 - White
   Ellen - female, age 20   Wood - male, age 11
   Jodie - female, age 18   Starks - male, age 8
   Callie - female, age 17   Addie - female, age 6
   Jonas - male, age 14

Harwood, J.W. - Range 3, Township 11 - White
   Alice - female, age 19   Edgar - male, age 9
   Sam - male, age 15   Annie - female, age 7
   Henry - male, age 11   Pearl - female, age 5

Hatton, J. - Range 2, Township 11 - White
   Lettie - female, age 18   Charley - male, age 10

Hatton, J. - Range 3, Township 11 - Colored
   Lillie - female, age 18   Chas - male, age 10

Hattox, C.C. - Range 2, Township 8 - White
   Jas - male, age 18   Zadie - female, age 11
   Emma - female, age 16   Walter - male, age 6
   Atwell - male, age 13   Effie - female, age 8

Hattox, J.B. - Range 1, Township 9 - White
   Belle - female, age 18   Jennie - female, age 8
   James - male, age 16   Lige - male, age 7
   Thos - male, age 13   Henry - male, age 5
   Mary - female, age 10

Hattox, J.H. - Range 3, Township 8 - White
   Jas - male, age 11   Ola - female, age 6
   Willie - male, age 11   Hilton - male, age 5
   Millard - male, age 8

Hawkins, W.B. - Range 2, Township 10 - White
    Amos - male, age 15   Amanda - female, age 10
    Alice - female, age 12

Hayes, J.M. - Range 2, Township 8 - White
    Bob - male, age 16   L.E. - female, age 8
    Lora - female, age 10

Hearn, J.C. - Range 1, Township 8 - White
    Lina - female, age 12   Joe - male, age 10

Hellums, A.M. - Range 1, Township 10 - White
    Walter - male, age 19   Lucy - female, age 10
    Fannie - female, age 14

Hellums, D.A. - Range 1, Township 11 - White
    Viola - female, age 16   Ace - male, age 10
    Wm - male, age 12   Walter - male, age 8

Hellums, I.N. - Range 1, Township 10 - White
    Florette - female, age 20   Daisy - female, age 9
    Lena - female, age 18   Lowry - male, age 6
    Coleman - male, age 16   Martha - female, age 5
    Russell - male, age 12

Hellums, S.W. - Range 1, Township 10 - White
    Arthur - male, age 14   John - male, age 9
    Dora - female, age 11   Jessie - female, age 7

Henderson, E. - Range 4, Township 11 - White
    Elbert - male, age 14   Eugene - female, age 12
    Vara - female, age 13

Henderson, W.J. - Range 4, Township 11 - White
    Willie - male, age 19   Ada - female, age 12
    Jessee - male, age 17   Robt - male, age 9
    Lucius - male, age 15   Alma - female, age 6

Hendricks, G.A. - Range 4, Township 11 - White
    Ed - male, age 11   Willie - male, age 6
    Milford - male, age 9

Hendricks, L.E. - Range 4, Township 11 - White
    Miller - male, age 9   Oscar - male, age 7

Helton, Pink - Range 3, Township 11 - White
    Kate - female, age 19   Cora - female, age 13
    Hattie - female, age 17   Lucian - male, age 10
    Daisy - female, age 15

Helton, T.W. - Range 2, Township 11 - White
    L.K. - female, age 18   D.T. - female, age 14
    L.H. - female, age 16   R.C. - female, age 11

Henderson, G.W. - Range 1, Township 10 - White
    Martha - female, age 18   Wm - male, age 16

Henderson, J.L. - Range 3, Township 10 - White
    Viola - female, age 17   Walter - male, age 10
    J.T. - male, age 15   Anna - female, age 7
    Eustace - male, age 12   Jessie - female, age 5

Henry, B.L. - Range 1, Township 11 - White
    Clarence - male, age 10   Mary - female, age 10
    Ada - female, age 11

Henry, J.F. - Range 2, Township 11 - White
    Tom - male, age 20   Alf - male, age 13

Herd, Fannie - Range 4, Township 11 - Colored
    Nellie - female, age 19   Simon - male, age 5
    Elbert - male, age 15

Herd, H.L. - Range, Township 10 - White
    A.E. - male, age 19   Amanda - female, age 14
    Flora - female, age 17   Henry - male, age 12
    M.G. - female, age 15   Bertha - female, age 9

Herd, Jno - Range 1, Township 11 - White
    Chas - male, age 12   Susie - female, age 6
    Lula - female, age 10   Claudie - female, age 5
    Ollie - female, age 8

Herd, Thos - Range 3, Township 10 - Colored
    Mary - female, age 17   Hart - male, age 9
    Curtis - male, age 16   Henry - male, age 7
    Jno - male, age 12   Geo - male, age 5
    Martha - female, age 10

Herdon, M. - Range 1, Township 10 - White
    Alice - female, age 16   Edit - male, age 5
    Pallas - female, age 7

Hereford, M. - Range 3, Township 9 - Colored
    Jetta - female, age 18

Hereford, Will - Range 3, Township 9 - Colored
    Chas - male, age 10   Lee - male, age 7

Herndon, N.E. - Range 1, Township 11 - White
    Sarah - female, age 20   Emma - female, age 14
    Oscar - male, age 19   Jas - male, age 12
    Martha - female, age 16

Heron, T.F. - Pontotoc - White
    Kate - female, age 16   Anna - female, age 12

Herring, J.M. - Range 1, Township 11 - White
    Polley - female, age 6

Herring, Orange - Range 3, Township 8 - Colored
    Emma - female, age 15   Eliza - female, age 16
    Wesly - male, age 17   Lora - female, age 12
    Geo - male, age 15

Hersey, J. - Range 4, Township 11 - White
    Word - male, age 17

Hersey, J. - Range 4, Township 11 - Colored
    Word - male, age 17   Walker - male, age 9
    Alf - male, age 12   Della - female, age 7

Hester, Celitia - Range 3, Township 11 - Colored
   Fannie - female, age 18   Alice - female, age 12
   Thos - male, age 16   Alma - female, age 9
   Sarah - female, age 17   Nelson - male, age 7
   Robt - male, age 14

Hester, H.C. - Range 4, Township 11 - White
   Joe - male, age 18   Lula - female, age 5

Hester, H.H. - Range 3, Township 11 - Colored
   Buck - male, age 8   Jno - male, age 7

Hester, Jas - Range 3, Township 9 - White
   Eva - female, age 14   Adolphus - male, age 10
   Smith - male, age 12

Hester, Jno - Range 4, Township 9 - Colored
   Sam - male, age 19   Jane - female, age 14
   Bettie - female, age 17   Caroline - female, age 12

Hester, W.H. - Range 4, Township 10 - White
   Neely - male, age 16   Mat - male, age 14

Hester, W.T. - Range 4, Township 11 - White
   Willie - male, age 11   Susie - female, age 8

Hewlett, H.R. - Range 1, Township 9 - White
   Estus - male, age 11   Clellan - male, age 7
   Duffie - male, age 10   Horace - male, age 5

Hickman, S.H. - Range 2, Township 8 - Colored
   Geo - male, age 16   Page - male, age 16
   Scott - male, age 7   Byanna - female, age 10

Higgins, J.H. - Range 2, Township 8 - White
   Anna - female, age 11

High, B.E. - Range 2, Township 9 - White
   E.B. - male, age 8

High, J.L. - Range 2, Township 9 - White
   Mary - female, age 10   Julia - female, age 9
   Martha - female, age 10   D.L. - male, age 5

High, Tom - Range 4, Township 10 - White
   Cena - female, age 7   Laura - female, age 6

High, Jake - Pontotoc - Colored
   Elvira - female, age 18   Linda - female, age 14
   Ed - male, age 10

Hightower, A. - Range 3, Township 11 - Colored
   Sam - age 6

Hill, A. - Range 4, Township 10 - Colored
   Harrison - male, age 8   Prude, Cora - female, age 20
   Lee - male, age 15

Hill, A.J. - Range 2, Township 9 - White
   W.P.L. - male, age 20   J.S.G. - male, age 11
   Mack - male, age 18   L.M. - female, age 7
   M.E. - female, age 16   Z.M. - male, age 6

Hill, A.J. - Range 1, Township 10 - White
    Mattie - female, age 20   Mat - female, age 16
    Lizzie - female, age 18   Andy - male, age 13
    Willie - male, age 5

Hill, Ed - Range 3, Township 8 - Colored
    Will - male, age 14   Jim - male, age 14

Hill, J.R. - Range 2, Township 8 - White
    W.T. - male, age 20   Guy - male, age 11
    Carrie - female, age 18   Ludie - female, age 9
    Estelle - female, age 16   Lula - female, age 6

Hill, M.H. - Range 4, Township 11 - Colored
    Wm - male, age 12   Jno - male, age 10
    Perry - male, age 11   Lillie - female, age 5
    Mary - female, age 9

Hill, Margaret - Range 3, Township 11 - Colored
    Wes - male, age 12   Rena - female, age 8
    Lou - female, age 10

Hinds, T.S. - Range 4, Township 11 - Colored
    Minnie - female, age 17   Jno - male, age 15
    Kate - female, age 13   Lizzie - female, age 11

Hinton, H.A. - Range 4, Township 11 - White
    R.B. - male, age 14   Jno - male, age 11

Hitchcock, Mack - Range 1, Township 11 - White
    Willie - male, age 10   Mary - female, age 8

Hitchcock, S.M. - Range 1, Township 11 - White
    Alice - female, age 18   Jno - male, age 15
    Emma - female, age 19   Kittie - female, age 13
    Frank - male, age 17   George - male, age 11

Hitt, J.M. - Guardian - Range 3, Township 9 - White
    Cruse, Geo - male, age 13

Hobson, Frank - Range 4, Township 10 - White
    Eve - female, age 18   Curt - male, age 14
    Thos - male, age 16

Hobson, J. - Range 3, Township 11 - Colored
    Wm - male, age 20   James - male, age 9
    Maggie - female, age 16   Frierson - male, age 7
    Georgia - female, age 13   Rosco - male, age 5
    Queen - male, age 9

Hobson, Jno - Range 4, Township 11 - Colored
    Lizzie - female, age 14   Van - male, age 8

Hobson, Peter - Range 3, Township 11 - Colored
    Anna - female, age 18   Lee - male, age 12
    Bettie - female, age 17   Emma - female, age 8
    Jno - male, age 10   Edgar - male, age 10

Hobson, Allen - Range 3, Township 11 - Colored
    Carry - female, age 17   Oliver - male, age 12

Hodges, B.F. - Range 1, Township 8 - White
    E.D. - male, age 18
    C.V. - male, age 16
    C.V. - female, age 14
    Tom - male, age 13
    Wyatt - male, age 12
    Frank - male, age 10
    Dovie - female, age 6

Hodges, E.H. - Range 4, Township 11 - Colored
    Allie - male, age 6
    Lou - male, age 5

Hodges, Ed - Range 4, Township 11 - Colored
    Henry - male, age 20
    Jack - male, age 16
    Lee - male, age 14

Hodges, G.W. - Range 2, Township 10 - White
    Clara - female, age 15
    Myrtle - female, age 13
    Bulah - female, age 11
    Abbie - female, age 9
    Clifton - male, age 7
    Clyde - female, age 5

Hodges, J.T. - Range 1, Township 10 - White
    Grover - male, age 6

Hodges, Jno = Range 4, Township 11 - Colored
    Jessie - female, age 17
    Lewis - male, age 14

Hodges, Will - Range 2, Township 8 - Colored
    Minnie - female, age 16
    Rush - male, age 12
    Sam - male, age 10
    Anna - female, age 8

Hodges, Wm - Range 1, Township 8 - White
    Thos - male, age 16
    Euna - female, age 10
    Wm - male, age 9
    Ester - female, age 6
    Nora - female, age 5

Holcomb, J.R. - Range 4, Township 9 - White
    Isam - male, age 17
    Mary - female, age 16
    Susie - female, age 14
    Geo - male, age 13
    Jno - male, age 9
    Alice - female, age 7

Holcomb, J.T. - Range 4, Township 10 - White
    Jno - male, age 7

Holcomb, Jas - Range 4, Township 10 - White
    Willie - male, age 9

Holland, Henry - Pontotoc - Colored
    Lizzie - female, age 19
    Jas - male, age 16
    Dowd - male, age 15
    Pink - male, age 13
    Amanda - female, age 10
    Jno - male, age 7
    Mary - female, age 7
    Matilda - female, age 5

Holland, J.H. - Range 4, Township 11 - White
    Lanie - female, age 14
    Mary - female, age 12
    Millie - female, age 10
    Henry - male, age 8
    Lewis - male, age 5

Holditch, J.D. - Range 3, Township 8 - White
    Jno - male, age 9
    Belva - female, age 7
    Lena - female, age 6

Holley, Joe - Range 4, Township 9 - Colored
    Ed - male, age 16
    Willie - male, age 14
    Henry - male, age 14

Holley, W.L. - Range 3, Township 11 - White
   Walter - male, age 9

Holliman, A.P. - Range 1, Township 9 - White
   Charley - male, age 17

Holloway, J.H. - Range 2, Township 11 - White
   Joe - male, age 15   Anderson - male, age 6
   Arthur - male, age 9

Holmes, W.B. - Range 4, Township 9 - White
   Florence - female, age 10   John - male, age 7
   Alma - female, age 9

Holmes, W.F., Jr. - Range 4, Township 9 - White
   Ethel - female, age 11   Gaston, male, age 5
   Belvelle - female, age 8

Homan, Issac - Range 4, Township 9 - White
   Pope, Ed - male, age 16   Pope, Alma - female, age 10
   Pope, Vardie - male, age 8

Homan, A.P. - Range 3, Township 8 - Colored
   Pitts, Bee - male age 17   Pitts, Fred - male, age 6
   Pitts, Nora - female, age 13

Homan, J.A. - Range 3, Township 9 - White
   Bettie - female, age 12   Pickens - male, age 8
   Sam - male, age 10   Fannie - female, age 6

Hooker, J.A. - Range 1, Township 9 - White
   Adison - female, age 12   Jerome - male, age 6
   Hadon - male, age 10   Viddo - female, age 5
   Hamilton - male, age 8

Hooker, J.C. - Range 2, Township 8 - White
   Gould - male, age 8   Gray - male, age 6

Hooker, W.P., Jr. - Range 2, Township 8 - White
   P.M. - male, age 10   Cornie - female, age 7
   Dean - male, age 8   Nellie - female, age 5

Horton, H.C. - Range 4, Township 10 - White
   Calvin - male, age 17   Need - male, age 14
   Martha - female, age 16

Horton, J.N. - Range 4, Township 11 - White
   Jenora - female, age 18   Lela - female, age 12
   Blanch - female, age 16   Effie - female, age 9
   Fred - male, age 14

Houpt, B.J. - Range 1, Township 11 - White
   Ben - male, age 11   Carry - female, age 6
   Pearl - female, age 10

Hoyle, B.F. - Range 2, Township 9 - White
   Allen - male, age 17   Cordie - female, age 9
   Edgar - male, age 13   Oscar - male, age 6
   Clara - female, age 11

Hoyle, C.M. - Range 1, Township 8 - White
   R.E.C. - female, age 19   M.E. - female, age 8
   M.D. - male, age 11

Hubbard, J.B. - Range 4, Township 9 - White
   Inezer - female, age 7   Rich'd - male, age 18

Hubbard, T.L. - Range 3, Township 10 - White
   Wm - male, age 19   Mattie - female, age 13
   Mollie - female, age 17   Thos - male, age 11
   Hortense - female, age 15   Jones - male, age 6

Hubbard, W.M. - Range 4, Township 9 - White
   Gus - male, age 15

Hudson, J.H. - Range 2, Township 8 - White
   Minnie - female, age 9   Annie - female, age 6

Hughes, C.M. - Range 3, Township 9 - White
   Onie - female, age 11

Hughey, J.M. - Range 4, Township 9 - White
   Willie - male, age 12   Sam - male, age 7
   Jno - male, age 10   Leona - female, age 5

Hughey, Jno - Range 2, Township 9 - White
   Walter - male, age 16   Virgil - male, age 8
   Edgar - male, age 15   Pearl - female, age 6
   Alma - female, age 10

Hutchison, H.R. - Range 3, Township 9 - White
   Lula - female, age 13   Ozie - female, age 9
   Stella - female, age 12   Ethel - female, age 8
   Zilpha - female, age 11   Lora - female, age 6

Hyde, A.C. - Range 3, Township 8 - Colored
   Willie - male, age 16   Mary - female, age 12
   Arthur - male, age 15   Vassie - male, age 9
   Andrew - male, age 13   Lula - female, age 5

Hyde, Dallas - Range 3, Township 9 - Colored
   Bulah - female, age 11   Anderson - male, age 6
   Jennie - female, age 9

Hyde, Jeff - Range 3, Township 9 - Colored
   Stanley - male, age 17   Al - male, age 13
   Mary - female, age 16   Henry - male, age 10
   Walter - male, age 14   Geo - male, age 9

Hyde, P. - Range 4, Township 10 - Colored
   Onie - female, age 20   Jane - female, age 10
   Ann - female, age 14   Luther - male, age 8
   M.R. - female, age 12

Hyde, W.B. - Range 2, Township 8 - White
   R.E. - male, age 19   Frank - male, age 12
   Mary - female, age 17   J.E. - male, age 10
   Edgar - male, age 14

Ingram, Elias - Range 3, Township 10 - Colored
   Frank - male, age 16   Wes - male, age 11
   Sarah - female, age 14   Jas - male, age 9
   Minnie - female, age 13   Fletcher - male, age 7
   Frances - female, age 12

Ingram, J.M. - Range 1, Township 11 - White
   Jno - male, age 14   Eva - female, age 5
   Lula - female, age 12

Ingram, J.M. - Range 1, Township 10 - White
   John - male, age 18   Emma - female, age 14
   Wm - male, age 12

Ingram, J.M. - Guardian - Range 1, Township 10 - White
   Luther, M. - male, age 9   Luther, Effie - female, age 7

Inman, J.F. Range 2, Township 10 - White
   Tavie - female, age 5

Inman, W.D. - Range 1, Township 10 - White
   Mollie - female, age 20   Lou - female, age 8
   Warner - male, age 18   Earle - female, age 7
   Ed - male, age 16   Wyatt - female, age 5
   Bettie - female, age 14   Wanzo - male, age 5
   Eugene - male, age 11

Isbell, Ad - Range 4, Township 11 - Colored
   Howard, Wes - male, age 19   Nathan, Joe - male, age 10
   Howard, Price - male, age 17   Williams, Ol - male, age 9
   Howard, Frank - male, age 13   Shannon, Rob - male, age 6
   Howard, Joe - male, age 10

Ivy, Isaac - Range 3, Township 10 - Colored
   Hattie - female, age 14   Della - female, age 12

Ivy, J.P. - Range 4, Township 11 - White
   Anna - female, age 16   Addie - female, age 8
   Luther - male, age 12   Archie - male, age 6

Jackson, Andrew - Range 4, Township 10 - Colored
   Andrew - male, age 18   Frank - male, age 15
   Carroll - male, age 17

Jackson, Chas - Guardian - Range 2, Township 8 - Colored
   Hooper, A.R. - male, age 12

Jackson, Hannah - Range 4, Township 8 - Colored
   James - male, age 18   Silas - male, age 12
   Willie - male, age 16   Bettie - female, age 10
   Robt - male, age 14   Modenia - female, age 6

Jackson, J.B.L. - Range 4, Township 11 - White
   R.H. - male, age 17   Marion - male, age 10
   Robt - male, age 15   Lula - female, age 8
   Jacob - male, age 14   Anna - female, age 7
   Josie - female, age 12   Lee - male, age 6

Jackson, J.H. - Range 2, Township 8 - White
   J.W. - male, age 19   L.L. - female, age 13
   F.E. - female, age 16

Jackson, Judson - Range 3, Township 9 - Colored
   Jno - male, age 8   Rich'd - male, age

Jackson, W.F. - Range 4, Township 10 - White
   Robt - male, age 8   Bessie - female, age 6

Jaggers, S.K. - Range 4, Township 11 - White
   Ann - female, age 19   Mary - female, age 13
   Lou - female, age 17   Luke - male, age 12
   Della - female, age 14   Sarah - female, age 9

James, W.L. - Range 1, Township 8 - White
   Isaac - male, age 8   Haydon - male, age 6

James, W.L. - Range 1, Township 8 - White
   Wm - male, age 19   Luther - male, age 14
   Tula - female, age 14   Pearl - female, age 10

Johnson, B.F. - Range 4, Township 11 - White
   Jas - male, age 6

Johnson, E.D. - Range 4, Township 10 - White
   Hattie - female, age 5

Johnson, J.O. - Range 4, Township 11 - Colored
   Dee - male, age 15   Jessie - female, age 7
   Cora - female, age 17

Johnson, J.L. - Range 4, Township 10 - White
   Wm - male, age 15   Eula - female, age 13

Johnson, J.T. - Range 4, Township 11 - White
   Geo - male, age 14   Lee - male, age 11
   Mack - male, age 11

Johnson, Jim - Range 4, Township 10 - Colored
   Geo - male, age 13   Lige - male, age 10

Johnson, Levi - Range 4, Township 10 - Colored
   Lula - female, age 17   Ada - female, age 8
   Lillie - female, age 11

Johnson, Mr. A.L. - Range 4, Township 10 - White
   Ida - female, age 16   Jas - male, age 14

Johnson, R.H. - Range 4, Township 10 - Colored
   Wm - male, age 17   Clark - male, age 9
   Alma - female, age 15   Edwards, Jake - male, age 13

Johnson, W.E. - Range 4, Township 11 - White
   Ed - male, age 16   Ara - female, age 10
   Jessie - female, age 14   Cleveland - male, age 8
   Leather - female, age 12   Hendrix - male, age 8

Johnson, W.N. - Range 4, Township 10 - White
   Daisy - female, age 8   Wm - male, age 6

Johnson, Simon - Range 4, Township - Colored
   Mary - female, age 10   Tilda - female, age 8

Jenkins, Frank - Range 3, Township 10 - Colored
   Wm - male, age 16   Minnie - female, age 8
   Chas - male, age 14   Garfield - male, age 5
   Peyton - male, age 11

Jenkins, J.A. - Range, Township 11 - White
   Ada - female, age 18   Annie - female, age 6
   Willie - male, age 13   Ella - female, age 7
   Harrison - male, age 12   Albert - male, age 5
   Jas - male, age 9

Jenkins, Jno - Range 3, Township 10 - White
   Lon - male, age 5

Jenkins, W.R. - Range 4, Township 10 - White
   Dottie - female, age 19   Willie - male, age 13
   Lewis - male, age 17   Maggie - female, age 10
   Walter - male, age 15   Pearle - female, age 8

Jamison, Mat - Pontotoc - Colored
   Will - male, age 20

Jernigan, G.W. - Range 2, Townsip 10 - White
   Lizzie - female, age 18   Dwight - male, age 10
   Ona - female, age 16   Hoyt - male, age 5
   Myrtle - female, age 12

Jernigan, J.H. - Range 2, Township 10 - White
   Watt - male, age 19   Maude - female, age 13
   Elma - female, age 17   Oscar - male, age 11
   Ed - male, age 15   Wiley - male, age 6

Jernigan, W.A. - Range 2, Township 10 - White
   Jas - male, age 17   Anna - female, age 8
   Chas - male, age 11   Ara - female, age 5

Jernigan, S.R. - Range 2, Township 10 - White
   Eva - female, age 10   Odelle - female, age 6
   Agnes - female, age 8

Johnson, C.W. - Range 1, Township 9 - White
   Jasper - male, age 6

Johnson, C.W. - Toccopola - White
   Wm - male, age 9   Joe - male, age 6
   Colley - male, age 7

Johnson, F. - Range 3, Township 10 - White
   Thos - male, age 9   Fannie - female, age 6
   Gus - male, age 8   Arnold, Miller - male, age 6

Johnson, H. - Range 3, Township 10 - Colored
   Frank - male, age 18   Lee - male, age 7
   Mose - male, age 12

Johnson, J.R. - Range 2, Township 11 - White
   Jno - male, age 17   Jessee - male, age 12
   Minnie - female, age 14

Johnson, J.S. - Range 3, Township 11 - White
   Rich'd - male, age 20   Robt - male, age 12
   Hattie - female, age 18   Lela - female, age 10
   Nettie - female, age 16   Lula - female, age 8

Johnson, Jas - Range 3, Township 8 - Colored
   Henry - male, age 11   John - male, age 5
   Hill - male, age 7

Johnson, L.B. - Range 3, Township 11 - White
   Horace - male, age 5   McWhorter, Jas - male, age 19

Johnson, L.H. - Range 3, Township 10 - White
   Gertie - female, age 5

Johnson, M.H. - Range 3, Township 10 - White
   Julia - female, age 18　　　　　　　Lillie - female, age 14
   Emma - female, age 16

Johnson, Mrs. M. - Range 3, Township 10 - White
   Jno - male, age 15　　　　　　　　Eugene - male, age 9
   Ed - male, age 12　　　　　　　　 Will - male, age 7

Johnson, Robert - Range 3, Township 11 - Colored
   Kittie - female, age 17　　　　　　Dora - female, age 7
   Lucy - female, age 14　　　　　　　Ellen - female, age 5
   Chas - male, age 13　　　　　　　　Nabors, Jno - male, age 8
   Bettie - female, age 11　　　　　　Nabors, Jeff - male, age 6
   Ed - male, age 9

Johnson, T.A. - Range 1, Township 11 - White
   Lee - male, age 18　　　　　　　　 Carry - female, age 14

Johnson, T.E. - Range 2, Township 11 - White
   Pearl - female, age 10　　　　　　 Earl - male, age 5
   Wm - male, age 7

Johnson, T.J. - Range 1, Township 9 - White
   Wm - male, age 11　　　　　　　　　Amanda - female, age 8
   Hugh - male, age 9

Johnson, Wm - Range 3, Township 11 - Colored
   Elon - male, age 9　　　　　　　　 Bradford - male, age 5
   Jas - male, age 8

Johnson, Wm - Range 3, Township 11 - White
   Jas - male, age 8

Johnson, Wm - Range 3, Township 11 - Colored
   Ellen - female, age 9　　　　　　　Bradford - male, age 5
   Jno - male, age 8

Jones, A.J. - Range 3, Township 10 - White
   Willie - male, age 16　　　　　　　Holt - male, age 8
   Daisy - female, age 15　　　　　　 Alvis - male, age 6
   Jas - male, age 12

Jones, Arthur - Range 4, Township 10 - Colored
   Mary - female, age 15　　　　　　　Dan - male, age 5
   Ida - female, age 9

Jones, D.J. - Range 3, Township 11 - White
   Mary - female, age 16　　　　　　　Word - male, age 7
   Ethel - female, age 13　　　　　　 Rush - male, age 5

Jones, F.A. - Range 1, Township 10 - White
   Wiley - male, age 12　　　　　　　 Jane - female, age 10

Jones, H. - Range 3, Township 11 - Colored
   P.E. - male, age 19　　　　　　　　Alf - male, age 7
   Maggie - female, age 15　　　　　　T.C. - male, age 20
   Lewis - male, age 11

Jones, J.N. - Range 3, Township 10 - White
   Pauline - female, age 11

Jones, R.B. - Range 4, Township 10 - White
   Walter - male, age 16   Jno - male, age 8
   Ida - female, age 14   Mattie - female, age 6
   Oscar - male, age 13   Lucy - female, age 5
   Emma - female, age 10

Jones, R.T. - Range 1, Township 10 - White
   Kittie - female, age 18   Jno - male, age 11
   Finis - male, age 14   Geo - male, age 8

Jones, R.T. - Guardian - Range 1, Township 10 - White
   Gregory, Josie - female, age 19

Jones, T.R. - Guardian - Range 1, Township 11 - White
   Hitchcock, Bettie - female, age 20   Gregory, Joe - male, age 14
   Gregory, Ju - male, age 18   Gregory, Geo - male, age 11
   Gregory, Venus - male, age 19

Jones, Taylor - Range 3, Township 10 - White
   Estelle - female, age 16   Arlena - female, age 11
   Walter - male, age 18   Bessie - female, age 7
   Anna - female, age 14   Judie - female, age 6

Jones, Taylor - Range 3, Township 11 - White
   Estelle - female, age 18   Arlena - female, age 11
   Walter - male, age 16   Bessie - female, age 7
   Ann - female, age 14   Judie - female, age 6

Jones, W.F. - Range 1, Township 10 - White
   Hosea - male, age 14   Berthea - female, age 10

Judson, Jas - Range 2, Township 8 - Colored
   Salina - female, age 11   Sam - male, age 6

Jumper, Tom - Range 2, Township 8 - White
   Wilmot - female, age 16   Coley - female, age 11
   Alice - female, age 14   Jas - male, age 8
                                       Lavada - female, age 6

Kelly, G.W. - Range 4, Township 9 - White
   Jas - male, age 13   Jake - female, age 6
   Etta - female, age 9

Kelly, J.J. - Range 4, Township 9 - White
   Clarence - male, age 6

Kelly, Mrs. M.J. - Range 4, Township 9 - White
   Oscar - male, age 18   Viola - female, age 12
   Oliver - male, age 17   Lucy - female, age 10
   Alice - female, age 14

Kelly, R.P. - Range 4, Township 8 - White
   Arthur - male, age 5

Kelly, Robt - Range 1, Township 11 - White
   Frank - male, age 5

Kelly, Robt - Guardian - Range 1, Township 11 - White
   Wysinger, Ed. - male, age 14

Kelly, T.S. - Range 4, Township 9 - White
   Geo - male, age 18   Lucy - female, age 11
   Jane - female, age 14

Kemp, H. - Range 4, Township 10 - Colored
- Prince - male, age 15
- Harriett - female, age 14
- Lee - female, age 12
- John - male, age 8
- Peter - male, age 7
- Emma - female, age 6

Kendrick, F.J. - Range 4, Township 11 - White
- A.L. - female, age 20
- E.P. - female, age 18
- L.E. - female, age 16
- Young - male, age 10

Kendrix, J. - Range 4, Township 9 - White
- Etta - female, age 18
- Ella - female, age 16
- Wm - male, age 10
- Ella - female, age 13
- Maggie - female, age 6

Kennedy, J.P. - Range 2, Township 10 - White
- Mary - female, age 17
- Jas - male, age 14
- Josie - female, age 12
- Ira - male, age 10
- Jane - female, age 8
- Era - female, age 7
- Ed - male, age 5

Key, Jesse - Range 1, Township 9 - Colored
- Lucian - male, age 13

Kidd, A.L. - Range 2, Township 9 - White
- Bascomb - male, age 6

Kidd, G.W. - Range 3, Township 10 - White
- Wm - male, age 16
- Nora - female, age 14
- Fannie - female, age 13
- Leanne - female, age 12
- Ludie - female, age 10
- Bessie - female, age 5

Kidd, J.T. - Range 2, Township 9 - White
- Agatha - female, age 10
- Delia - female, age 8
- Willie - female, age 6

Kidd, W.H. - Range 2, Township 9 - White
- Minnie - female, age 9
- Mart - male, age 7
- Lee - male, age 5

King, Henry - Range 3, Township 11 - Colored
- P.E. - male, age 19
- A.L. - female, age 16
- Willie - male, age 11
- J.H. - female, age 8
- Susie - female, age 17

King, J.D. - Range 4, Township 11 - White
- Ophelia - female, age 13
- Ed - male, age 8
- Sam - male, age 6

King, J.D. - Range 4, Township 10 - White
- Wm - male, age 18
- Joe - male, age 13
- Robt - male, age 12
- Lillie - female, age 8
- Gilbert - male, age 6

King, M.R. - Range 4, Township 9 - White
- Robt - male, age 20
- Isaac - male, age 18
- Edward - male, age 15
- Lena - female, age 9
- Jones - male, age 5

King, R.F. - Range 4, Township 10 - White
- Lora - female, age 15
- Frank - male, age 13
- Rich'd - male, age 10
- Zula - female, age 8
- Cleo - male, age 6

King, W.A. - Range 4, Township 11 - White
    Effie - female, age 9

Kingsley, J.W. - Troy - White
    Florence - female, age 18   Carroll - male, age 12
    Allie - female, age 16   Kate - female, age 10

Knight, John - Range 3, Township 8 - White
    Fannie - female, age 8

Knox, I.N. - Range 3, Township 9 - White
    Bruce - male, age 17   Dewit - male, age 10
    Ada - female, age 15   Alma - female, age 7
    Rush - male, age 12   I.C. - male, age 5

Knox, J.A. - Range 3, Township 10 - White
    J.R. - male, age 12   Albert - male, age 8
    H.D. - male, age 10   Robt - male, age 6

Kyle, J.R. - Guardian - Range 1, Township 9 - White
    Orr, Mattie - female, age 15

Kyle, R.A. - Range 1, Township 9 - White
    Anna - female, age 17

Lackey, Caleb - Range 4, Township 8 - White
    Preston- male, age 9

Lamar, E.P. - Range 1, Township 11 - White
    Wallace - male, age 18   Mollie - female, age 11
    Dollie - female, age 16   Victor - male, age 7
    Richard - male, age 14   Maggie - female, age 5

Lamar, W.W. - Range 1, Township 11 - White
    F.L. - female, age 5

lambert, J.L. - Range 4, Township 10 - White
    Jno - male, age 17   Mary - female, age 8
    Wm - male, age 10   L.T. - male, age 6
    Rachael - female, age 10

Lambert, J.T. - Range 4, Township 10 - White
    Chas - male, age 17   J.E. - male, age 12
    J.T. - male, age 17   A.E. - male, age 9
    J.M. - male, age 15   J.W. - male, age 6
    Ed - male, age 14

Lancaster, W.A. - RAnge 1, Township 11 - White
    Clyde - female, age 9   Mary - female, age 7

Langley, E.N. - Pontotoc - White
    Lizzie - female, age 16   Noble - male, age 10

Lantrip, Mrs. L.C. - Range 2, Township 10 - White
    John - male, age 18   Jas - male, age 12
    Frances - female, age 15

Laprade, W.B. - Range 3, Township 9 - White
    Arthur - male, age 15

Lauderdale, B.W. - Range 3, Township 11 - White
    W.T. - male, age 11   E.G. - female, age 8
    Robt - male, age 10

Lauderdale, J.R. - Range 4, Township 11 - White
   Elbert - male, age 12

Lauderdale, W.B. - Range 4, Township 11 - White
   Thos - male, age 10   Ed - male, age 7
   Vivla - female, age 8   Lillie - female, age 5

League, J.H. - Guardian - Range 4, Township 9 - White
   Blakely, Hattie - female, age 20

Lee, J.P. - Range 1, Township 11 - White
   Minnie - female, age 11   Carry - female, age 6

Leland, T.B. - Range 3, Township 9 - White
   Lovie - female, age 20

Lemons, J.C. - Range 2, Township 9 - White
   Lela - female, age 6

Leslie, Jim - Range 4, Township 9 - White
   Ab - male, age 15   Robt - male, age 7
   Jno - male, age 13   Marion - male, age 5
   Vincent - male, age 9

Leslie, R.W. - Range 4, Township 11 - White
   Thos - male, age 11   Amanda - female, age 8
   Anna - female, age 20   Jno - male, age 7

Levell, B.F. - Range 3, Township 9 - White
   Lela - female, age 17   Madge - female, age 10
   Dick - male, age 15   Katie - female, age 8
   Annie - female, age 12   Albert - male, age 6

Lewelling, B. - Range 2, Township 11 - White
   Wm - male, age 16   Charley - male, age 8
   Warren - male, age 13   Jennie - female, age 5
   Julia - female, age 11

Lewelling, B.F. - Range 1, Township 11 - White
   Walter - male, age 12   C.L. - male, age 15
   Gordon - male, age 10   E.L. - male, age 5

Lewelling, W.J. - Range 1, Township 10 - White
   Cora - female, age 9   Jno - male, age 7

Lilly, J.L. - Range 4, Township 9 - White
   Darden - male, age 14   Lillie - female, age 10
   James - male, age 13

Lindsay, Tom - Range 4, Township 11 - Colored
   Oscar - male, age 16

Lindsey, Abe - Range 4, Township 10 - White
   Robert - male, age 11   Lee - male, age 6
   Jno - male, age 8

Lindsey, W.M. - Range 1, Township 10 - White
   Wm - male, age 19   Calvin - male, age 11
   Moses - male, age 17   Ester - male, age 6

Lions, W.W. - Range 3, Township 9 - White
   Wiley - male, age 12   Annie - female, age 11
   Addie - female, age 16

Lissenbee, A.R. - Range 1, Township 9 - White
   Georgia - female, age 18   Alanda - male, age 12
   Ollie - female, age 14   Jennie - female, age 10
   Asborn - male age 19   Lillie - female, age 6

Little, A.J. - Range 4, Township 10 - White
   Sallie - female, age 19   Geo - male, age 10
   Elizabeth - female, age 16   Mary - female, age 5
   Jno - male, age 14

LIttle, A.M. - Range 4, Township 10 - White
   Eula - female, age 11   Jessee - male, age 6
   Robt - male, age 8

Little, H. - Range 4, Township 10 - White
   Jas - male, age 19   Bessie - female, age 15
   Geo - male, age 17   Jno - male, age 13
   Ella - female, age 14

Little, J. - Range 4, Township 8 - White
   Joe - male, age 14   McKnight, Lee - male, age 14

Little, J.C. - Range 4, Township 9 - White
   Thos - male, age 16   Seth - male, age 8
   Peyton - male, age 14   Zella - female, age 8
   Albert - male, age 11   Norman - male, age 6

Little, W.R. - Range 4, Township 9 - White
   Chas - male, age 8   Duke, Sallie - female, age 13
   Jas - male, age 5   Duke, Thos - male, age 8
   Duke, Robt - male, age 18   Duke, Ella - female, age 7
   Duke, Luther - male, age 17

Littlejohn, J.C. - Range 3, Township 8 - White
   Morris - male, age 19   Walter - male, age 5
   Jasper - male, age 14   Lula - female, age 18
   Willie - male, age 13   Ella - female, age 16

Lockhart, G.W. - Range 4, Township 9 - White
   Claud - male, age 18   Fannie - female, age 14
   Emma - female, age 16   Lucy - female, age 11

Lockhart, J.E. - Range 4, Township 9 - White
   Walter - male, age 17   Edna - female, age 15

Lockley, Dave - Range 1, Township 10 - White
   Jas - male, age 17   Sam - male, age 10
   Dave - male, age 12   Susie - female, age 8

Long, Geo - Range 4, Township 11 - Colored
   Ed - male, age 6

Long, J.F. - Range 2, Township 9 - White
   Bessie - female, age 19   J.L. - female, age 14
   E.E. - female, age 17   L.D. - male, age 11
   R.K. - Male, age 16   E.B. - female, age 9

Long, J.K. - Range 2, Township 10 - White
   Jno - male, age 17   Tom - male, age 8
   Robt - male, age 14   Eddie - male, age 5

Long, T.J. - Range 2, Township 9 - White
   Bessie - female, age 19
   E.L. - male, age 17
   Rebecca - female, age 15
   J.L. - male, age 12
   L.D. - ,male. age 10
   E.B. - male, age 8
   Dy - male, age 6

Longest, Mrs. S.L. - Range 3, Township 11 - White
   Chris - male, age 20
   Jas - male, age 18
   Mayo, Judson - male, age 14
   Mayo, Eva - female, age 12
   Mayo, Katie - female, age 10

Love, Jno - Range 4, Township 9 - White
   Vera - female, age 5

Lower, M.J. - Range 2, Township 11 - White
   Chas - male, age 19
   Robt - male, age 17
   Susie - female, age 16
   York - male, age 11
   Harry - male, age 9

Lowry, C. - Range 4, Township 10 - White
   Daisy - female, age 12
   Retta - female, age 8
   Fletcher - male, age 6

Lowry, G.W. - Range 4, Township 10 - White
   Verna - male, age 10
   Winford - male, age 7
   Zera - female, age 5

Lowry, Jas - Range 3, Township 10 - White
   Resinia - female, age 11
   Wm - male, age 19
   Cora - female, age 7
   Viola - female, age 6
   Emma - female, age 5

Lowry, Julia - Pontotoc - Colored
   Lena - female, age 16

Lowry, Mat - Range 4, Township 10 - Colored
   Lou - female, age 16
   Willie - male, age 12

Lowry, Mrs. M.J. - Range 3, Township 10 - White
   A.A. - male, age 18
   B.O. - male, age 14
   R.C. - female, age 16
   J.M. - male, age 13

Lowry, W.N. - Range 4, Township 10 - White
   Wm - male, age 15
   Essie - female, age 11
   Birdie - female, age 9
   Erskin - male, age 6

Lowry, W.P. - Range 3, Township 10 - White
   M. - female, age 19
   Alma - female, age 13
   C. - female, age 11

Lowry, W.T. - Range 1, Township 8 - White
   Lawrence - male, age 19
   Lonnie - male, age 18
   Levy - male, age 16
   Martha - female, age 12
   Eva - female, age 5

Lyon, Easter - Range 3, Township 10 - Colored
   Allen - male, age 16
   Lena - female, age 13
   Joe - male, age 10
   Manda - female, age 8
   Jim - male, age 7
   Sallie - female, age 5

Lyon, T.J. - Range 3, Township 9 - White
   Alise - male, age 17
   Charles - male, age 15
   Jeff - male, age 13
   Cruse, Maggie female, age 17

McAmey, Buck - Range 4, Township 11 - Colored
   Mary - female, age 12   Mattie - female, age 15
   Willie - male, age 6   Ella - female, age 13
   Kate - female, age 5

McAmey, Jas - Range 4, Township 11 - Colored
   Buck - male, age 17   Chas - male, age 12
   Jettie - male, age 5

McAshan, Francis - Range 3, Township 10 - Colored
   Chas - male, age 17   Mary - female, age 11
   Mattie - female, age 14   Hattie - female, age 8

McCarter, G.A. - Range 1, Township 9 - White
   Robt - male, age 11   Hattie - female, age 15
   John - male, age 13   Lucy - female, age 17

McCarter, H.S. - Range 2, Township 9 - White
   Cordelia - female, age 16   Brewster - male, age 13

McCarter, J.R. - Range 2, Township 9 - White
   Arlenie - female, age 18

McCarver, Mack - Range 2, Township 9 - White
   Lula - female, age 12   Jno - male, age 8
   Vernon - male, age 10   Sallie - female, age 5

McCary, Z.T. - Range 1, Township 10 - White
   Martin - male, age 16   Robt - male, age 9
   Wiley - male, age 11   Nora - female, age 7

McCharen, J.H. - Range 1, Township 10 - White
   Edna - female, age 16   Nora - female, age 9
   Walter - male, age 13   Jno - male, age 7
   Callis - female, age 11   Lillie - female, age 5

McCharen, R.E. - Range 1, Township 9 - White
   Alma - female, age 19   Bertie - female, age 7
   Sample - male, age 18   Burt - male, age 7
   Jane - female, age 17   Lillian - female, age 5

McCluskey, I.M. - Range 3, Township 11 - White
   Guy - male, age 10   Trimia - female, age 8

McClusky, M.J. - Range 2, Township 11 - White
   V.G. - male, age 10   Thos - male, age 8

McCollough, D.S. - Range 2, Township 11 - White
   J.P. - male, age 20   Nannie - female, age 13
   Claude - male, age 18   D.J. - male, age 12
   Sam - male, age 16   L.J. - male, age 10
   I.M. - female, age 15   Susie - female, age 8

McCollugh, J.R. - Range 1, Township 9 - White
   Arthur - male, age 18   Margaret - female, age 10
   Anna - female, age 14   Katie - female, age 12

McCollough, S.D. - Range 3, Township 11 - White
   Lena - female, age 20   Jessie - female, age 9
   Sam - male, age 18   Spence - male, age 8
   Georgia - female, age 16   Sallie - female, age 6
   Ida - female, age 15   Nortie - male, age 13
   James - male, age 12

McConnell, R.M. - Range 4, Township 11 - Colored
   Jno - male, age 17   Lucy - female, age 14
   Alex - male, age 15   Mariah - female, age 8

McCord, J.D. - Range 4, Township 9 - White
   Robt - male, age 12   Daisy - female, age 10

McCord, J.M. - Range 3, Township 10 - White
   Thos - male, age 12   Sallie - female, age 7
   Cornelius - male, age 19   Maggie - female, age 5

McCord, Jessee - Range 3, Township 9 - Colored
   Lorene - female, age 13   Robt - male, age 6
   Jno - male, age 9   Lavender - male, age 5

McCord, Lewis - Pontotoc - Colored
   Jennie - female, age 14   Sallie - female, age 10

McCord, R.B. - Range 1, Township 11 - White
   Ed - male, age 18   Oscar - male, age 12
   Wallace - male, age 16   Ernest - male, age 7

McCord, W.N. - Range 4, Township 9 - White
   Rural - male, age 10   Cora - female, age 7
   Sim - male, age 5

McCoy, A.S., Sr. - Range 4, Township 9 - White
   Jno - male, age 19

McCoy, G.W. - Range 3, Township 8 - White
   Lawrence - male, age 13   Cora - female, age 7
   Maud - female, age 11   Nellie - female, age 5

McCoy, J.E. - Range 2, Township 10 - White
   Minnie - female, age 10   Jettie - female, age 6
   Jennie - female, age 8

McCoy, J.M. - Range 4, Township 9 - White
   Bonie - female, age 10   Clarence - male, age 5
   Fronie - female, age 8

McCoy - Range 2, Township 10 - White
   Alf - male, age 13   Minnie - female, age 8
   Walter - male, age 11

McCoy, S.S. - Range 3, Township 8 - White
   Willie - male, age 17   Fannie - female, age 10
   Minnie - female, age 16

McCraw, L.R. - Range 4, Township 8 - White
   Jessee - male, age 9   Eula - female, age 5
   Chester - male, age 7

McCraw, B.A. - Range 4, Township 8 - White
   Lydia - female, age 9   Millie - female, age 5
   Bessie - female, age 7

McDaniel, E.C. - Range 1, Township 9 - White
   John - male, age 18   Sam - male, age 14

McDonald, J.T. - Range 2, Township 9 - White
   Hattie - female, age 16

McDowell, J.T.B. - Range 3, Township 8 - White
    Sallie - female, age 19   Fannie - female, age 12
    Mamie - female, age 17   Lillie - female, age 10
    Ada - female, age 15   Lydia - female, age 8

McEachen, J.W. - Range 2, Township 9 - White
    Doyle - male, age 5

McEachern, J.W. - Range 1, Township 9 - White
    O. - female, age 20   Charley, male, age 19

McGaughty, Robt - Range 4, Township 9 - Colored
    Hayes - male, age 14   Dewit - male, age 8
    Clifton - male, age 10

McGee, C. - Range 2, Township 11 - White
    Willie - male, age 16   John - male, age 8
    Ed - male, age 14   Anna - female, age 5

McGill, J.W. - Range 4, Township 11 - White
    Jas - male, age 10   Emma - female, age 8

McGonagill, J.D. - Range 1, Township 10 - White
    Wm - male, age 20   Hubbard - male, age 13
    Clara - female, age 18

McGregor, E. - Range 1, Township 10 - White
    Lewis - male, age 18   Vera - female, age 10
    J.H. - male, age 16   Zona - female, age 7
    Zora - female, age 12   Zola - female, age 5

McGregor, G. - Range 1, Township 10 - White
    Jas - male, age 20   Rebecca - female, age 14
    Willis - male, age 18   Geo - male, age 12
    Wiley - male, age 16   Eddie - male, age 7

McGregor, J.J. - Range 1, Township 10 - White
    Stanford - male, age 19   Jennie - female, age 11
    Emma - female, age 17   Joe - male, age 7
    Harrison - male, age 16   Mary - female, age 5
    Frank - male, age 14

McGregor, W. - Range 1, Township 10 - White
    Geo - male, age 12   Minnie - female, age 8
    Willie - male, age 10

McGregor, W.W. - Range 1, Township 10 - White
    Nathan - male, age 17   Walter - male, age 15
    Bud - male, age 16

McKinney, R. - Range 4, Township 11 - Colored
    Mary - female, age 19   E.C. - male, age 5
    D.E. - female, age 8

McKnight, D.W. - Range 3, Township 8 - White
    Alice - female, age 20   Ethel - female, age 7
    Carry - female, age 18   Ben - male, age 16
    Ida - female, age 17   Thos - male, age 13
    Etta - female, age 12   Ellis - male, age 14
    Ada - female, age 8   Zack - male, age 10

McKnight, R.N. - Range 2, Township 11 - White
    Bettie - female, age 18   Ophelia - female, age 14
    Ida - female, age 16   Wm - male, age 12
    Rich'd - male, age 15

McKnight, S.B. - Range 3, Township 11 - White
    M.J. - male, age 17   Willie - male, age 19
    Sam - male, age 15   Minnie - female, age 6

McLarty, Wm - Range 1, Township 9 - White
    Eddie - male, age 16   Berthea - female, age 7

McMillan, Ed - Range 4, Township 8 - Colored
    Jessee - male, age 5   John - male, age 10
    Annie - female, age 13

McMillan, J.F. - Range 4, Township 9 - White
    Jas - male, age 12   Willie - male, age 8
    Jno - male, age 10   Peter - male, age 5

McNeal, L. - Range 2, Township 9 - White
    Tessue - female, age 11

McNeal, S.D. - Range 4, Township 8 - White
    Cypert, Maud - female, age 20   Cypert, Emma - female, age 15

McNeely, J.L. - Range 1, Township 9 - White
    J.A. - male, age 17

McVey, Mrs. M.A. - Range 1, Township 11 - White
    Walter - male, age 19

McWhorter, J.M. - Range 2, Township 11 - White
    Bettie - female, age 18   Robt - male, age 10
    Josie - female, age 16   Chas - male age 11
    Lottie - female, age 12   Clelland - male age 6

McWhorter, J.T. - Range 3, Township 11 - White
    Ellie - female, age 9   David - male, age 5
    Aggie - female, age 7

McWhorter, J.T. - Range 2, Township 11 - White
    Elva - female, age 9   Davis - male, age 5
    Agnes - female, age 6

McWhorter, R.L. - Range 2, Township 11 - White
    Anna - female, age 7

McWhorter, W.H. - Range 2, Township 11 - White
    N.T. - male, age 18   R.L. - male, age 13
    M.E. - female, age 16   Wallace - male, age 11

Maddox, G.U. - Range 4, Township 8 - White
    Ed - male, age 6

Mahan, E.C. - Range 1, Township 9 - White
    Alice - female, age 19   Maud - female, age 14
    Sprugeon - male, age 11

Maize, Caroline - Pontotoc - Colored
    Roxie - female, age 15   Susie - female, age 5
    Wm - male, age 13

Malone, Allen - Range 4, Township 10 - Colored
   Clark - male, age 18   Sallie - female, age 13
   Rayman - male, age 18   Lizzie - female, age 6
   Jno - male, age 13

Malone, Ann - Range 3, Township 11 - Colored
   Jno - male 11   Chas - male, age 18
   Ann - female, age 8

Malone, C.N. - Range 4, Township 10 - White
   Mitchell, male, age 12   Bulah - female, age 8
   Ed - male, age 10   Thos - male, age 6

Malory, Fannie - Range 4, Township 11 - Colored
   Henry - male, age 9   Maud - female, age 5
   Lizzie - female, age 7

Malory, Fannie - Range 4, Township 11 - Colored
   Wyle - male, age 14   Hattie - female, age 9
   Arthur - male, age 13   Eddie - male, age 6

Malory, J.D. - Range 4, Township 11 - White
   Mary - female, age 13   Jessee - male, age 9
   Annie - female, age 11   Maud - age 6

Manahan, A.J. - Range 4, Township 10 - White
   Willie - male, age 11

Marion, Henry - Range 3, Township 11 - Colored
   John - male, age 16   Mollie - female, age 10
   Bob - male, age 15   Clarence - male, age 8
   Lula - female, age 12   Lonnie - male, age 6

Marion, Henry - Range 3, Township 11 - Colored
   Jas - male, age 16   Mollie - female, age 10
   Robt - male, age 14   Clarence - male, age 8
   Lou - female, age 12   Neal, Lou - male, age 6

Marshall, J.M. - Guardian - Range 4, Township 9 - White
   Bean, Geo - male, age 18

Martin, M. - Range 1, Township 11 - White
   Maud - female, age 9   Will - male, age 6
   Jim - male, age 7   Geo - male, age 5

Martin, M.D. - Range 1, Township 9 - White
   Dwight - male, age 6

Martin, M.S. - Range 1, Township 10 - White
   Ida - female, age 19   Sim - male, age 9
   Ed - male, age 16   Luther - male, age 7
   Tilla - female, age 11   Jno - male, age 5

Martin, R.Q. - Range 3, Township 9 - White
   Callie - female, age 13   Gus - male, age 10
   Mattie - female, age 13

Martin, Sam - Range 4, Township 11 - White
   Sarah - female, age 10   Julia - female, age 8

Mask, A.B. - Range 2, Township 10 - White
   Florence - female, age 16   Bettie - female, age 10
   Elias - male, age 13   Margaret - female, age 5
   Victoria - female, age 12

Massey, J.N. - Toccopola - White
   Florence - female, age 17   Elliott - male, age 11
   Lindsay - male, age 16   Willie - male, age 7
   Lovie - female, age 13   Susie - female, age 5

Mathews, James - Range 1, Township 9 - White
   Hugh - male, age 13   Erskin - male, age 6
   Jettis - male, age 7

Mathews, W.H. - Range 4, Township 11 - White
   Jno - male, age 18   Lula - female, age 10
   Lem - male, age 17   Henry - male, age 8
   M.I. - female, age 13   Lon - male, age 5
   Zella - female, age 12

Matkins, I.Z. - Range 1, Township 9 - White
   Nancy - female, age 10   Ada - female, age 9
   Lucy - female, age 16   Lee - male, age 7
   Willie - male, age 11

Mattox, L.T. - Range 2, Township 9 - White
   Villa - female, age 12

Mauldin, Mrs. M.C. - Range 3, Township 11 - White
   Ottey - male, age 14

May, S.E. - Range 2, Township 10 - White
   Wes - male, age 16   Sue - female, age 14

Mayfield, Geo - Range 4, Township 8 - Colored
   Luther - male, age 8   Prudie - male, age 12
   Lula - female, age 14   Frances - female, age 9
   Ella - female, age 15   Sula - female, age 5

Mayfield, H. - Range 4, Township 11 - Colored
   Lee - male, age 13   Daisy - female, age 9
   Lewis - male, age 12   Violet - female, age 7

Mayhew, J.A. - Range 1, Township 9 - White
   Jessie - female, age 15   Buss - male, age 7
   Ben - male, age 11   Ivy - male, age 6

Mayo, J.T. - Range 3, Township 11 - White
   E.E. - female, age 19   S.T. - male, age 15

Mayo , J.T. - Range 2, Township 11 - White
   J.S. - male, age 20   T.S. - female, age 15
   Lizzie - female, age 18

Maze, W.F. - Guardian - Range 2, Township 9 - White
   Rutledge, Junior - male, age 16

Medlock, W.H. - Range 4, Township 9 - White
   Geo - male, age 15   Bill - male, age 8
   Elizabeth - female, age 12   May - female, age 5
   Maggie - female, age 10

Medly, B. - Range 4, Township 9 - Colored
    Tine - male, age 7

Memlin, Jno - Range 1, Township 11 - White
    Tom - male, age 17
    Joe - male, age 13
    Jas - male, age 10
    Jno - male, age 8
    Geo - male, age 6

Meyers, S.D. - Troy - White
    E.R. - male, age 10
    W.H. - male, age 5

Milam, H.P. - Range 3, Township 9 - White
    Jno - male, age 20
    Bell - female, age 17
    Luna - female, age 15
    Carry - female, age 13
    Emma - female, age 11
    Andrew - male, age 8
    Grover - male, age 6

Milam, J.W. - Range 3, Township 9 - White
    Jno - male, age 18

Milam, W.A. - Range 2, Township 9 - White
    Ora - female, age 11
    Madie - female, age 10
    Thos - male, age 8
    Era - female, age 6

Millender, E.H. - Pontotoc - White
    Hannah - female, age 15

Miller, Froney - Range 3, Township 11 - Colored
    Ed - male, age 15
    Lillian - female, age 12

Miller, I.T. - Range 3, Township 10 - White
    Jessie - female, age 9
    Herman - male, age 6

Miller, J.A. - Range 1, Township 11 - White
    Dora - female, age 11
    Jack - male, age 7

Miller, J.L. - Range 2, Township 10 - White
    John - male, age 18
    Jas - male, age 13
    Ida - female, age 16
    Kate - female, age 10
    Jeannette - female, age 8

Miller, James - Range 3, Township 8 - Colored
    Lige - male, age 10

Miller, Jane - Pontotoc - Colored
    Will - male, age 7
    Susie - female, age 5

Miller, Lewis - Range 4, Township 9 - Colored
    Martha - female, age 15
    Mary - female, age 12
    Will - male, age 18
    Robt - male, age 10
    Jno - male, age 5

Miller, Pat - Pontotoc - Colored
    Duncan, Geo - male, age 10

Miller, Pat - Range 3, Township 9 - Colored
    Wm - male, age 18
    Bill - male, age 7

Miller, S.M. - Range 3, Township 11 - Colored
    D. - male, age 5

Miller, Sam - Range 3, Township 9 - Colored
    Frank - male, age 15
    Lon - male, age 12
    Ed - male, age 9
    Lorenzo - male, age 6
    Jno - male, age 5

Mills, J.T. - Range 4, Townhip 8 - White
   Geo - male, age 15

Milsap, Taylor - Range 3, Township 8 - White
   Frank - male, age 5

Milsap, Taylor - Range 3, Township 8 - Colored
   Amanda - female, age 15   Cass - male, age 7
   Emma - female, age 11

Milstead, Frank - Range 4, Township 11 - White
   Claudie - female, age 6

Mitchell, A. - Range 3, Township 9 - Colored
   Chas - male, age 8   Ada - female, age 6

Mitchell, C.B. - Pontotoc - White
   Geo - male age 17   Ida - female, age 5
   Anna - female, age 15   Patterson, Josie - female age 5

Mitchell, J.A. - Range 1, Township 11 - White
   Panie - female, age 18

Mitchell, L.R. - Range 1, Township 10 - White
   Mallie - female, age 18   Misher - male, age 13
   Maggie - female, age 16   Lena - female, age 10

Mitchell, W.F. - Range 4, Township 8 - White
   Bettie - female, age 17   Mary - female, age 9
   James - male, age 12   Ellen - female, age 6

Montgomery, C.M. - Range 1, Township 9 - White
   Maggie - female, age 16   Addie - female, age 9
   Alada - female, age 12   Tom - male, age 7

Montgomery, C.L. - Range 3, Township 10 - White
   Ada - female, age 17

Montgomery, G.A. - Range 3, Township 10 - White
   Chas - male, age 18   Alice - female, age 15

Montgomery, H. - Range 4, Township 10 - White
   Mary - female, age 8   Wm - male, age 6

Montgomery, J.C. - Range 3, Township 10 - White
   Chester - male, age 7   Jas - male, age 5

Montgomery, Mrs. Fannie - Range 2, Township 10 - White
   Logan - male, age 20   Joe - male, age 14
   Dock - male, age 18   Andrew - male, age 6
   Mattie - female, age 16

Montgomery, R.H. - Range 3, Township 10 - White
   Wesly - male, age 15   Frank - male, age 8
   Andrew - male, age 13   Florence - female, age 6
   Walter - male, age 10

Montgomery, T.E. - Range 3, Township 11 - White
   Irene - female, age 17   Carrie - female, age 10
   Goode - male age 14   Susie - female, age 8
   Elvira - female, age 12

Montgomery, W.R. - Range 4, Township 9 - White
   Geo - male, age 18　　　　　　　　Emma - female, age 9
   Jno - male, age 15　　　　　　　　Jennie - female, age 7
   Jo - male, age 12　　　　　　　　　Lena - female, age 5

Montgomery, W.A. - Range 1, Township 11 - White
   Nancy - female, age 15　　　　　　Elma - female, age 12
   Katie - female, age 14　　　　　　Pearl - female, age 6

Montgomery, W.B. - Range 3, Township 10 - White
   Hugh - male, age 16　　　　　　　 Willie - male, age 9
   Dave - male, age 12

Moore, B.L. - Toccopola - White
   J.W. - male, age 19　　　　　　　 J.S. - male, age 13
   O.C. - male, age 17　　　　　　　 M.M. - female, age 9
   Jno - male, age 15　　　　　　　　T.L. - male, age 6

Moore, Mrs. A.H. - Range 2, Township 10 - White
   Jennie - female, age 20　　　　　 Willie - male, age 16
   Thos - male, age 18

Moore, Mrs. Nannie - Range 3, Township 10 - White
   James - male, age 14　　　　　　　Dude - male, age 10
   Gus - male, age 13　　　　　　　　Bennie - male, age 9
   Robt - male, age 11　　　　　　　 Senie - female, age 7

Moore, Harriett - Range 1, Township 9 - Colored
   Henry - male, age 12　　　　　　　Mittie, female, age 12
   Anderson, male, age 10　　　　　　Harden, Lizzie female, age 12

Moore, J.H. - Range 3, Township 11 - White
   Wm - male, age 14　　　　　　　　 Jo - male, age 8
   Jno - male, age 12　　　　　　　　Maggie - female, age 6
   Jessee - male, age 10

Moore, Mrs. - Range 1, Township 10 - Colored
   Henry - male, age 12　　　　　　　Mattie - female, age 12
   Andy - male, age 10　　　　　　　 Lizzie - female, age 12

Moore, Nancy - Range 4, Township 11 - Colored
   Tom - male, age 10　　　　　　　　Jane - female, age 15

Moore, P. - Range 2, Township 11 - Colored
   H.W. - male, age 18　　　　　　　 Lydia - female, age 14
   W.J. - male, age 19　　　　　　　 Lewis - male, age 8
   M.E. - male, age 16

Moore, Rich - Range 3, Township 11 - Colored
   Tuck - male, age 9　　　　　　　　Williams, Lena - female, age 5
   Belle - female, age 11　　　　　　Williams, Geo - male, age 9

Moore, Sarah - Range 2, Township 9 - White
   E.D. - male, age 17　　　　　　　 R.T. - male, age 14

Moore, W.D. - Range 2, Township 10 - White
   Annie - female, age 17　　　　　　Martha - female, age 13
   Jas - male, age 15　　　　　　　　Andrew - male, age 11

Moore, W.H. - Range 4, Township 11 - White
   Jno - male, age 10　　　　　　　　Mollie - female, age 8

Morman, James - Range 4, Township 9 - White
   Geo - male, age 18
   Dan - amle, age 12
   Jno - male, age 8
   Oscar - male, age 5
   Silas - male, age 7
   Wilder, Emma female, age 17

Morphis, J.L. - Range 2, Township 11 - White
   Peter - male, age 19
   Hugh - male, age 17
   Sallie - female, age 15
   Grace - female, age 13
   Jessie - female, age 10
   Chas - male, age 8
   Lonzo - male, age 6

Morris, Richard - Range 4, Township 11 - Colored
   Rosa - female, age 7

Morris, W.J. - Range 1, Township 8 - White
   Martha - female, age 12
   Sarah - female, age 10
   Pearl - female, age 6

Morrison, M. - Range 2, Township 9 - White
   Jno - male, age 18
   L.A. - male, age 14
   C.A. - male, age 12
   Claud - male, age 10
   Nora - female, age 15
   Arthur - male, age 5

Morrow, E.G. - Range 4, Township 11 - White
   Lucy - female, age 16
   Thos - male, age 9

Morrow, J.A. - Toccopola - White
   Dovie - female, age 7
   I.E. - female, age 5

Mounce, M.L. - Range 3, Township 8 - White
   Geo - male, age 19
   Walter - male, age 17
   Mary - female, age 16
   Maggie - female, age 15
   Susie - female, age 12
   Willie - male, age 6

Munn, J.A. - Guardian - Range 4, Township 9 - Colored
   Woods, Willie - male, age 5

Munn, J.B. - Range 4, Township 10 - White
   Thos - male, age 18
   Geo - male, age 15
   Sam - male, age 9
   Clifton - male, age 6

Murphy, W.G. - Range 1, Township 11 - White
   Lena - female, age 14
   Susie - female, age 12
   Lon - male, age 10
   Gid - male, age 8
   Lucy - female, age 6

Myers, S.D. - Range 4, Township 11 - White
   E.K. - female, age 10
   W.H. - male, age 5

Myers, Till - Range 4, Township 10 - White
   Etta - female, age 16
   Georgia - female, age 14
   Simon - male, age 12
   Arthur - male, age 10
   Andrew - male, age 8
   Babe - male, age 6

Nabors, Frank - Range 3, Township 11 - Colored
   Anna - female, age 7

Nathan, Alf - Range 4, Township 11 - Colored
   Dora - female, age 19
   Robt - male, age 16
   Irene - female, age 12
   Gus - male, age 14
   Minnie - female, age 8
   Katie - female, age 7
   Dena - female, age 6

Naugher, W.T. - Range 3, Township 10 - White
   Jno - male, age 13   Carry - female, age 8
   Clara - female, age 8   Auby - male, age 5

Neal, J.D. - Range 2, Township 10 - White
   Daisy - female, age 11   Ollie - female, age 7
   Sallie - female, age 10   Aggy - female, age 5
   Sam - male, age 9   Parrish, G.L. - male, age 17

Neal, Lee - Range 1, Township 10 - White
   Claud - male, age 8

Neal, Wesly - Range 3, Township 8 - Colored
   Frank - male, age 18   Crew - male, age 11
   Mary - female, age 15   Ada - female, age 8
   Ester - female, age 12   Dee - male, age 6

Nelson, A.C. - Range 1, Township 9 - White
   Nora - female, age 15   Charley - male, age 11
   Ebbott - male, age 13   Willie - male, age 9

Nelson, Mrs. E. - Range 4, Townhip 11 - White
   Lillie - female, age 18   Passie - female, age 13
   Willie - male, age 17   Lee - male, age 11
   Sudie - female, age 16   Mattie - female, age 8

Nelson, Robt - Range 1, Township 10 - White
   Sallie - female, age 17   Julia - female, age 14

Nelson, T.J. - Pontotoc - White
   Howard - male, age 11

New, E. - Range 1, Township 9 - White
   Hattie - female age 15   Sarah - female, age 8
   Sam - male, age 12   Tom - male, age 6
   Milton - male, age 10

New, E. - Guardian - Range 1, Township 9 - White
   Cummings, Anna - female, age 12   Cummings, Jno - male, age 7

New, W.M. - Range 1, Township 8 - White
   Zollie - female, age 9   Alice - female, age 7
   Dolie - female, age 7   John - male, age 5

Newell, D.J. - Range 1, Township 9 - White
   Green - male, age 10   Loyce - female, age 5
   Wm - male, age 7

Newell, W.B. - Range 1, Township 9 - White
   Baxter - male, age 6

Newell, W.J. - Range 2, Township 10 - White
   Baker - male, age 20   Claud - male, age 8
   Chas - male, age 16   Preston - male, age 6
   Darden - male, age 12

Nisbet, J.M. - Pontotoc - White
   Wm - male, age 12   Lula - female, age 10
   Mamie - female, age 8   Lena - female, age 5

Nisbet, Lee - Range 3, Township 9 - Colored
   Hattie - female, age 11   Lena - female, age 5
   Hannah - female, age 8

Nixon, E.B. - Range 3, Township 9 - White
   Robt - male, age 12   Jno - male, age 9

Norman, Lige - Range 3, Township 10 - Colored
   Clara - female, age 15   Eliza - female, age 9
   John - male, age 13   Julia - female, age 6
   Rose - female, age 11

Norwood, Phillip - Range 4, Township 9 - Colored
   Walter - male, age 15   Pearl - female, age 6
   Willie - male, age 13   Desert - male, age 9
   Corintha - female, age 11   Earl - male, age 5
   Pauline - female, age 9

Norwood, Sam - Range 4, Township 9 - Colored
   Lucy - female, age 13   Henry - male, age 5
   Cenie - female, age 7

Nowlin, U.C. - Range 1, Township 9 - White
   Nancy - female, age 17   Minnie - female, age 8
   Sarah - female, age 13   Lettie - female, age 6
   Pearl - female, age 11

Nowlin, W.C. - Range 2, Township 9 - White
   Chas - male, age 15   Robt - male, age 13
   Mary - female, age 16   Myrtle - female, age 10

Oakes, A.B. - Range 2, Township 9 - White
   Dora - female, age 13   Jno - male, age 10
   Georgia - female, age 11   Amey - female, age 6

O'Calligan, W.H. - Range 4, Township 9 - White
   Clyde - male, age 6   Emma - female, age 5

O'Claligan, Jas - Range 4, Township 9 - White
   Wm - male, age 12   Jno - male, age 8
   Mattie - female, age 10   Sam - male, age 6

Odle, J.J. - Range 2, Township 10 - White
   Etta - female, age 9   Alama - female, age 5

Oliver, Katie - Range 3, Township 10 - White
   Alf - male, age 9   Delma - female, age 6

Oliver, Kate - Range 4, Township 11 - White
   S.L. - male, age 9   W.M. - male, age 7

O'Neal, Jas - Range 4, Township 10 - Colored
   Felix - male, age 16   Jas - male, age 9
   Hannah - female, age 12   Westmoland, Burrell - male, age 17

Orr, Jno - Range 4, Township 9 - Colored
   Mazella - female, age 9

Owen, Alex - Range 3, Township 9 - White
   Harrison - male, age 14   Geo - male, age 10
   Jno - male, age 12   Judge - male age 8

Owen, G.A. - Guardian - Range 4, Township 9 - White
   Graham, Ed - male, age 15

Owen, G.A. - Range 4, Township 9 - White
   Mary - female, age 18   Lillie - female, age 12
   Maggie - female, age 17   Annie - female, age 8

Owen, J.B. - Range 4, Township 10 - White
   Maybel - female, age 10   Estelle - female, age 9
   Clara - female, age 8

Owen, J.P. - Range 2, Towsnhip 10 - White
   Hardy - male, age 19   Ara - female, age 12
   Joe - male, age 17   Susie - female, age 10
   Alf - male, age 16   Sina - female, age 8
   Jas - male, age 14   Brady - male, age 5

Owen, Mrs. H. - Range 2, Township 11 - White
   Henry - male, age 19

Owen, Mrs. H. - Range 3, Township 11 - White
   Henry - male, age 19

Owen, R.H. - Range 1, Township 9 - White
   Cora - female, age 18   Robt - male, age 12
   Nannie - female, age 14

Owen, Warren - Range 3, Township 8 - Colored
   May - female, age 14

Pack, Wesly - Range 4, Township 11 - Colored
   Sol - male, age 19   Elzy -male, age 14
   Jno - male, age 18   Emily - female, age 12
   Frances - female, age 16   Mary - female, age 9

Palmer, R.F. - Range 3, Township 10 - White
   Leona - female, age 16   Julia - feamale, age 10
   Carry - female, age 14   Maggie - female, age 8
   Robt - male, age 12   Nathan - male, age 5

Pannell, E.M. - Range 4, Township 11 - White
   Carrie - female, age 17   Fred - male, age 11
   May - female, age 15

Pannell, S.M. - Range 4, Township 11 - White
   Rich'd - male, age 17   Jane - female, age 8
   Robt - male, age 15   Ludella - male, age 5

Pannell, W.E. - Range 3, Township 11 - White
   Rufus - male, age 18   Ellie - female, age 10
   Monroe - male, age 15   Minnie - female, age 8
   Robt - male, age 12

Pannell, W.E. - Range 4, Township 11 - White
   W.R. - male, age 17   Ellen - female, age 10
   J.M. - male, age 15   Minnie - female, age 8
   R.L. - male, age 13

Pappasan, J.M. - Range 1, Township 11 - White
   Jas - male, age 20   Ida - female, age 16
   Murphy - male, age 18

Parrish, Chas - Pontotoc - Colored
   Jessie - male, age 17   Chas - male, age 15

Parrish, J.F. - Range 4, Township 9 - White
   Will - male, age 14   Ellen - female, age 11
   Celia - female, age 12   Jno - male, age 17

Parrish, J.M. - Range 2, Township 9 - White
   W.L. - male, age 19   Sulia - female, age 15
   Valentine - male, age 17   Bettie - female, age 13

Parrish, Mary - Pontotoc - Colored
   Wm - male, age 6

Parrish, Wm - Range 3, Township 10 - Colored
   Chas - male, age 14

Parks, H. - Range 1, Township 9 - Colored
   Henry - male, age 11   Lula - female, age 11
   John - male, age 13   Julia - female, age 9

Parks, W.T. - Range 4, Township 8 - White
   Walter - male, age 19   Amanda - female, age 15
   Jim - male, age 12   Maggie - female, age 14
   Barnett - male, age 9

Parrish, C.C. - Range 4, Township 10 - White
   Jas - male, age 18   Lula - female, age 12
   Wm - male, age 16   Ora - female, age 10
   Allie - male, age 14   Sallie - female, age 8

Paschal, S.A. - Toccopola - White
   Carl - male, age 7   S.E. - female, age 5

Patterson, A.J. - Range 1, Township 8 - White
   Viola - female, age 14   Luther - male, age 8
   Jane - female, age 13   Omie - female, age 6
   Toney - male, age 11

Patterson, J.A. - Range 2, Township 10 - White
   Lillie - female, age 16   Irene - female, age 8
   Guy - male, age 14   George - male, age 6
   Ida - female, age 10   Annie - female, age 5

Patterson, J.R. - Range 1, Township 9 - White
   A.C. - male, age 17   Earl - male, age 6
   L.N. - female, age 13   Pearl - female, age 6
   Edward - male, age 10

Patterson, M.A. - Range 1, Township 9 - White
   M.P. - male, age 19   Ida - female, age 12
   T.E. - male, age 16   Wm - male, age 11
   T.C. - female, age 14   R.R. - male, age 11
   E.V. - female, age 15   L.G. - male, age 5

Patterson, N.A. - Range 2, Township 10 - White
   T.R. - male, age 18   Frank - male, age 15

Patterson, T.P. - Range 1, Township 9 - White
   Rastus - male, age 14   Maude - female, age 7
   Festus - male, age 12   Best - male, age 5
   Chester - male, age 10

Patterson, W.A. - Range 2, Township 10 - White
   Ester - female, age 8   Robt - male, age 6

Payne, Frank - Range 3, Township 11 - White
   Susie - female, age 15   Mollie - female, age 9
   Jane - female, age 11   Lewis - male, age 7

Payne, J.I. - Range 3, Township 10 - White
   Willie - male, age 18

Payne, J.S. - Guardian - Range 4, Township 9 - White
   Cox, Ida - female, age 17   Cox - female, age 18
   Cox, Dock - male, age 14

Peachy, J. - Range 1, Township 10 - White
   Maggie - female, age 16   James - male, age 12

Peden, A.A. - Range 3, Township 11 - White
   Isalena - female, age 17   Waddil - male, age 10
   John - male, age 14   Frierson - male, age 7

Peden, Lucy - Range 2, Township 11 - White
   Jas - male, age 11   C.E. - male, age 9

Pegues, Alf - Range 3, Township 9 - Colored
   Ben - male, age 15   Sylvester - male, age 9

Pegues, E.C. - Pontotoc - White
   Anna - female, age 10   May - female, age 7
   Jno - male, age 8

Pegues, Easter - Range 2, Township 9 - Colored
   Will - male, age 17   Maud - female, age 10
   Arthur - male, age 14

Pegues, W.B. - Range 3, Township 9 - Colored
   Henry - male, age 16

Pegues, W.R. - Pontotoc - White
   Nellie - female, age 8   Chas - male, age 5

Perry, Chas - Range 3, Township 11 - White
   Wm - male, age 15   Rush - male, age 11
   Jno - male, age 14   Nora - female, age 10
   Eliza - female, age 13   Sim - male, age 9
   Vallie - female, age 12   Carry - female, age 6

Perry, A.M. - Range 4, Township 10 - White
   Willis - male, age 10   Lou - female, age 8

Perry, Dock - Range 2, Township 8 - Colored
   Savannah - female, age 12   Bettie - female, age 7
   Orlena - female, age 11

Perry, P. - Range 4, Township 11 - White
   Wm - male, age 19   Tilden - male, age 8
   Hulda - female, age 16

Petiet, H. - Range 1, Township 11 - White
   Sarah - female, age 17   Baswell - male, age 12
   Columbus - male, age 19   Nathan - male age 10
   Ada - female, age 15

Petiet, J.C. - Range 4, Township 11 - White
   Edna - female, age 14   Idelle - female, age 7
   Sam - male, age 12   Craig - male, age 5
   Thos - male, age 9

Petiet, J.J. - Range 2, Township 11 - White
   Nora - female, age 7   Leona - female, age 5

Petiet, W.W. - Range 1, Township 11 - White
    Arthur - male, age 8   Lora - female, age 5

Phife, Ed - Range 2, Township 10 - Colored
    Eddie - male, age 5

Phifer, J.D. - Range 2, Township 9 - White
    Lillian - female, age 6

Phillips, Aaron - Range 1, Township 11 - White
    Lynn - male, age 18   Bettie - female, age 10
    Sarah - female, age 12

Phillips, J.A. - Range 2, Township 10 - White
    Jno - male, age 20   Walter, male, age 13
    Geo - male, age 17   Van - male, age 10
    Paul - male, age 15   Mary - female, age 5

Phillips, J.N. - Range 2, Township 9 - White
    John - male, age 18   Walter - male, age 10
    Sam - male, age 16   M.Y. - female, age 5
    Gus - male, age 14

Phillips, Mrs. N.C. - Range 1, Township 11 - White
    Flora - female, age 12

Pickens, E.M. - Range 1, Township 10 - White
    Donnie - female, age 19   Bulah - female, age 7
    Lena - female, age 14   Lela - female, age 5
    Luckey - female, age 12

Pickens, N.E. - Range 4, Township 10 - White
    M.I.C. - male, age 17   J.E. - male, age 10
    Josephine - female, age 15   L.D. - male, age 7
    M.L. - female, age 13

Pickens, W.S. - Range 1, Township 9 - White
    Earnest - male, age 9   Tura - female, age 5
    J.E. - male, age 7

Pickens, W.S. - Guardian - Range 1, Township 9 - White
    Blackstock, Henry - male, age 18   Blackstock, Luster - male, age 9
    Blackstock, Joe - male, age 14   Blackstock, Alice - female, age 10

Pilcher, J.S. - Range 2, Township 9 - White
    Henry - male, age 9   Gertrude - female, age 5
    Mattie - male, age 6

Pinson, Ed - Range 3, Township 10 - Colored
    Frank - male, age 9   Sim - male, age 5
    Arthur - male, age 7

Pinson, L. - Range 3, Township 9 - White
    Robt - male, age 8   Frank - male, age 7

Pinson, Rachael - Range 3, Township 10 - Colored
    Lizzie - female, age 18   Green - male, age 13
    Ada - female, age 16   Lewis - male, age 10

Pittman, J.L. - Range 1, Township 8 - White
    Emma - female, age 18   Melia - female, age 9
    Isa - female, age 15   Andrew - male, age 8
    Newt - male, age 14   Cora - female, age 5
    Oscar - male, age 10   Carrie - female, age 5

Pitts, A.H. - Range 3, Township 9 - White
   Walter - male, age 15   Ethel - female, age 8
   Alta - female, age 13   Claud - male, age 6
   Aubray - male, age 12

Pitts, C.L. - Range 3, Township 10 - White
   Martha - female, age 19   Modena - female, age 14
   Minnie - female, age 16   Carry - female, age 12

Pitts, Charlotte - Range 3, Township 8 - Colored
   Walter - male, age 18   Lou - female, age 11
   Ann - Female, age 19   Ervin - male, age 5

Pitts, D.E. - Range 3, Township 9 - Colored
   Hugh - male, age 18   Florence - female, age 16
   Vester - male, age 12   Lou - female, age 18
   Dan - male, age 10

Pitts, D.T. - Range 3, Township 8 - White
   Laura - female, age 17

Pitts, G.W. - Range 2, Township 9 - Colored
   Birdie - female, age 5

Pitts, H.W. - Range 3, Township 8 - White (written in pencil Mother)
   Eddie - male, age 13   Carry - female, age 8
   Laura - female, age 11   Irene - female, age 5
   Nora - female, age 10

Pitts, J.F. - Range 3, Township 8 - White
   Luther - male, age 16   Burr - male, age 9
   Oscar - male, age 13   Maggie - female, age 6
   Ben - male, age 11

Pitts, J.W. - Range 3, Township 8 - White
   Whit - male, age 7   Lula - female, age 5

Pitts, Lee - Range 3, Township 8 - Colored
   Bee - male, age 16   Claudie - female, age 12
   Givan - male, age 14   Roy - male, age 9

Pitts, M.B. - Pontotoc - White
   Lillie - female, age 8   Miller - male, age 5
   Katie - female, age 7

Pitts, P.P. - Range 2, Township 9 - Colored
   Cora - female, age 14

Pitts, R.L. - Range 3, Township 8 - White
   Annie - female, age 20   Carry - female, age 12
   Mary - female, age 18   Mattie - female, age 12
   Leona - female, age 16   John - male, age 20
   Sam - male, age 14

Pitts, Robt - Range 3, Township 9 - White (written in pencil Grandfather)
   Jno - male, age 17

Pitts, W.C. - Range 3, Township 9 - White
   Wm - male, age 12   Nora - female, age 14
   Minnie - female, age 18   Addie - female, age 9

Pitts, W.H. - Range 3, Township 10 - White
   Walter - male, age 14   Bulah - female, age 5
   Mary - female, age 12

Plant, G.W. - Range 3, Township 9 - Colored
   Georgia - female, age 10   Julia - female, age 5
   Wm - male, age 8

Pitts, W.R. - Range 3, Township 9 - White
   Arthur - male, age 19   Montee - female, age 10
   Dee- female, age 16

Polk, E.A. - Range 2, Township 10 - White
   Will - male, age 18   Jeff - male, age 10
   Oscar - male, age 16   Pearl - female, age 8

Polk, J.F. - Range 3, Township 11 - White
   Sallie - female, age 18   Frank - male, age 10
   Jas - male, age 15   Ernest - male, age 7

Polk, Jno - Range 4, Township 11 - Colored
   Rose - female, age 5

Polk, S.M. - Range 1, Township 9 - White
   Earnest - male, age 15   Ben - male, age 7
   Eula - female, age 13   Dovie - female, age 7
   Fonsy - male, age 11

Ponder, J.W. - Range 4, Township 9 - White
   Wesly - male, age 17   Leanna - female, age 11
   Joe - male, age 5   Pearl - female, age 8
   Mallie - female, age 13   Sarah - female, age 6

Pope, J.B. - Range 4, Township 10 - White
   J.B. - male, age 18

Pope, J.F. - Range 3, Township 10 - White
   Maud - female, age 18   Jno - male age 9
   Singleton - male, age 13   Edna - female, age 9
   Harriett - female, age 11

Porter, L.E. - Range 4, Township 11 - White
   Nep - male, age 11   Luther - male, age 8
   Fred - male, age 10   Rube - male, age 5

Porter, W.M. - Range 1, Township 11 - White
   Robt - male, age 7   Neely - female, age 5

Potts, W.H. - Range 4, Township 11 - White
   Dees, Claudie - female, age 12   Dees, Henry - male, age 6

Pound, G.H.G., Jr. - Range 4, Township 9 - White
   Frank - male, age 5

Pound, J.M. - Range 4, Township 9 - White
   Willie - male, age 17   Roxie - male, age 10
   Herstler - male, age 12   Birdie - female, age 8

Powell, G.F. - Range 3, Township 10 - White
   Mattie - female, age 6

Powell, J.L. - Range 3, Township 8 - White
   Walter - male, age 18   Cora - female, age 12
   Wiley - male, age 16

Powell, J.M. - Guardian - Range 4, Township 8 - White
    Billingsley, Chas - male, age 16   Billingsley, Anna - female, age 13

Powell, J.M. - Range 4, Township 8 - White
    Miller - male, age 16   Carry - female, age 13
    Clarence - male, age 10   Jennie - female, age 6
    Etta - female, age 18

Powell, J.P.S. - Toccopola - White
    L.R. - male, age 18   Mullins, Minnie - female, age 10
    M.A. - female, age 13   Mullins, Nannie - female, age 10

Powell, L.R. - Guardian - Range 3, Township 11 - White
    Cannon, Sam - male, age 18

Poyner, J.R. - Range 2, Township 10 - White
    Nathan - male, age 6

Poyner, T.R. - Range 2, Township 10 - White
    Henry - male, age 8   Irene - female, age 5

Poyner, T.R. - Guardian - Range 2, Township 10 - White
    Vance, S. - male, age 10

Poyner, T.R. - Guardian - Range 2, Township 10 - White
    Ridge, Harvy - male, age 18

Price, Isaac - Toccopola - White
    Luther - male, age 18   Bourbon - male, age 9
    Lillie - female, age 16   Estelle - female, age 16

Price, Will - Range 1, Township 10 - White
    Isaac - male, age 6

Priest, J.P. - Troy - White
    Ada - female, age 18   Sallie - female, age 13
    Lillie - female, age 19   Verner - male, age 8
    Lula - female, age 16   Maggie - female, age 5
    Robt - male, age 15

Priest, J.T. - Range 4, Township 11 - White
    Mattie - female, age 13   Thos - male, age 7
    Mary - female, age 9   Nebraska - male, age 5

Priest, R.W. - Range 4, Township 11 - White
    Jas - male, age 15   Sallie - female, age 10
    Robt - male, age 12   Alva - female, age 6

Prince, J.R. - Range 1, Township 9 - White
    Willie - male, age 15   Viola - female, age 7

Pritchard, J.C. - Range 1, Township 11 - White
    Restima - female, age 7   Tempie - female, age 5

Pritchard, P.C. - Range 1, Township 11 - White
    Lula - female, age 16   Estus - female, age 7
    Eula - female, age 15   Adeline - female, age 7
    Lizzie - female, age 9

Pritchard, R.E. - Range 4, Township 9 - White
    Willie - male, age 17   Bulah - female, age 10
    Pink - male, age 15   Alice - female, age 8
    Nellie - female, age 13   Annie - female, age 5

Pritchard, R.J. - Range 4, Township 9 - White
   Ellen - female, age 19   Burney - female, age 8
   Susan - female, age 17   Sam - male, age 5
   Robt - male, age 13

Pritchard, S.P. - Range 2, Township 11 - White
   Ida - female, age 13   Ann - female, age 9
   Etta - female, age 11   Edna - female, age 5

Prude, Jo - Range 4, Township 11 - Colored
   Jno - male, age 19

Prude, L.A. - Range 3, Township 10 - Colored
   Annie - female, age 19   Lou - female, age 12
   Jennie - female, age 16

Prude, Rose - Range 4, Township 10 - Colored
   Jno - male, age 18   Lula - female, age 11
   Martha - female, age 16   Pink - male, age 5
   Joe - male, age 15   Willie - male, age 7
   M.I. - female, age 13

Prude, Shed - Range 3, Township 10 - Colored
   Susie - female, age 17   Amora - female, age 15
   Anna - female, age 17   Peter - male, age 13

Prude, Shed - Range 3, Township 11 - Colored
   Susan - female, age 17   Lucy - female, age 15
   Ann - female, age 16   Jno - male, age 13

Pruitt, V.G. - Range 2, Township 10 - White
   Chas - male, age 19   Boyd - male, age 9
   Willie - male, age 13   Annie - female, age 5
   Floyd - male, age 9   Jessie - female, age 5

Pulliam, J.W. - Range 3, Township 11 - White
   R.A. - male, age 15   S.I. - female, age 9
   J.M. - male, age 13   E.C. - female, age 7
   J.L. - male, age 6

Pulliam, Wm - Range 4, Township 11 - Colored
   Jack - male, age 18   Carry - female, age 14
   Eddie - male, age 16   Lena - female, age 6

Purdon, L.A. - Range 1, Township 10 - White
   Nathan - male, age 20   Lizzie - female, age 12
   Egbert - male, age 17   Maggie - female, age 9
   Nora - female, age 14

Purdon, Mrs. S.D. - Range 1, Township 10 - White
   Jeff - male, age 19   Henry - male, age 13
   Lou - female, age 20   Thos - male, age 11
   Robt - male, age 16   Jane - female, age 8

Purdon, Wm - Range 1, Township 10 - White
   Lou - female, age 16   Ora - female, age 12
   Sarmthia - female, age 14   Carter - male, age 8
   Ida - female, age 14

Purvine, D.S. - Range 2, Township 10 - White
   Sallie - female, age 17   Geo - male, age 8
   Mollie - female, age 15   West - male, age 8
   Aris - male, age 13   Lena - female, age 6
   Josie - female, age 12

Pyle, D.W. - Range 1, Township 9 - White
   Rosa - female, age 17   Ed - male, age 9
   Charley - male, age 16   Luther - male, age 5
   Anna - female, age 14

Rackley, E. - Range 4, Township 11 - White
   Adelle - female, age 7   Mary - female, age 5

Rackley, Jno - Range 4, Township 11 - White
   Mary - female, age 9   Gillespie, Thos - male, age 17
   Lottie - female, age 7   Gillespie, Wm - male, age 17
   Erb - male, age 5

Rackley, Mrs. M.F. - Range 4, Township 11 - White
   Ben - male, age 18   Lottie - female, age 12
   Rube - male, age 16   Carry - female, age 11
   Lucian - male, age 9

Randall, A.L. - Range 2, Township 9 - White
   Jas - male, age 19   Lewis - male, age 11
   Josie - female, age 17   Bettie - female, age 9
   Thos - male, age 10

Raper, T.A. - Range 4, Township 11 - White
   Ida - female, age 6   Clifford - male, age 8
   David - male, age 10

Ray, R.F. - Pontotoc - White
   M.J. - female, age 18

Ray, J.S. - Range 4, Township 9 - White
   Frazier - male, age 13   Monetta - female, age 6
   Carrie - female, age 10

Ray, W.A. - Range 2, Township 10 - White
   Marlin - male, age 6

Rayburn, Mrs. E.O.M. - Toccopola - White
   Katie - female, age 19   Qubelle - female, age 13
   Jno - male, age 18

Rea, J.H. - Range 1, Township 10 - White
   Chalmers - male, age 11

Rea, Jno - Range 2, Townhip 10 - White
   Tom - male, age 18   Mattie - female, age 16

Reed, J. - Guardian - Range 4, Township 8 - White
   Smith, Enoch - male, age 14   Chatman, Flora - female, age 13
   Chatman, Perry - male, age 14   Chatman, Etta - female, age 11

Reed, Lewis - Range 3, Township 11 - Colored
   Susie - female, age 6

Reed, Luther - Range 2, Township 9 - Colored
   Alice - female, age 15   Geo - male, age 10
   Fannie - female, age 13   Elihu - male, age 9
   Julia - female, age 12   Margaret - female, age 8

Reed, Russell - Range 4, Township 11 - White
   Mamie - female, age 17   Elon - male, age 14

Reeder, I.L. - Range 1, Township 11 - White
   Archie - male, age 7   Maud - female, age 5

Reeder, J.C. - Range 4, Township 10 - White
   Cordia - female, age 6

Reeder, J.E. - Range 2, Township 11 - White
   Earl - male, age 15   Nannie - female, age 7
   Elon - male, age 10

Reeder, W.R. - Range 4, Township 11 - White
   M.I. - male, age 18   Minnie - female, age 8
   Jodie - female, age 17   Lillie - female, age 6
   Jno - male, age 10   Arthur - male, age 5
   Jas - male, age 8

Reid, Frances - Range 4, Township 11 - Colored
   Henry - male, age 10   Dennis - male, age 5
   Geo - male, age 8

Reid, Randall - Range 4, Township 11 - Colored
   Bettie - female, age 18   Jane - female, age 14

Reno, Andrew - Range 3, Township 9 - Colored
   Alice - female, age 5

Reno, Calvin - Range 3, Township 9 - Colored
   Ed - male, age 15   Lorena - female, age 10
   Wes - male, age 13   Hattie - female, age 10
   Sallie - female, age 12

Renno, Daniel - Range 2, Township 9 - Colored
   Lou - female, age 17   Arthur - male, age 11
   Mary - female, age 14   Dan'l - male, age 8
   Ida - female, age 12   Geo - male, age 5

Reno, Neal - Range 3, Township 10 - Colored
   James - male, age 16   Rich'd - male, age 8
   Willie - male, age 14   Alice - female, age 6
   Lizzie - female, age 12   Bolton, Martha - female, age 14
   Chas - male, age 10

Reynolds, J.C. - Range 2, Township 10 - White
   Mary - female, age 17   Luna - female, age 11
   Matilda - female, age 16   Susie - female, age 8
   Luvilla - female, age 13   Lillie - female, age 6

Rhodes, Thos - Range 4, Township 11 - White
   Mattie - female, age 19   Lewis - male, age 14
   Love - female, age 17   Della - female, age 11
   Lum - male, age 16   Ida - female, age 7

Richards, J.H. - Range 2, Township 11 - White
   Martha - female, age 9   Salitia - female, age 6
   Eugene - male, age 6

Riddle, W.A. - Range 4, Township 11 - White
   Wm - male, age 19   Anna - female, age 12
   Jno - male, age 16   Des - male, age 10
   Sarah - female, age 14   Lucius - male, age 8

Ridge, Mrs. N.A. - Range 2, Towsnhip 10 - White
   Harvy - male, age 18　　　　　　　Nannie - female, age 14
   Joe - male, age 16　　　　　　　　Flora - female, age 9
   Wallace - male, age 15　　　　　　Ella - female, age 19

Ridling, Mrs. Ann - Range 1, Township 10 - White
   Almond - male, age 11　　　　　　 Thos - male, age 8

Riley, M. - Range 1, Township 8 - White
   Edward - male, age 13　　　　　　 Levi - male, age 10
   Wm - male, age 13　　　　　　　　 Dosie - female, age 5
   Lonnie - male, age 11

Robins, J.A. - Range 4, Township 8 - White
   Chas - male, age 17　　　　　　　 Dollie - female, age 12
   Ella - female, age 19　　　　　　 Callie - female, age 10
   Azie - female, age 16　　　　　　 Maggie - female, age 7

Robbins, B. - Range 1, Township 9 - White
   Henry - male, age 20　　　　　　　Joe - male, age 17
   Wiley - male, age 18　　　　　　　Foster - male, age 10

Robbins, D.B. - Range 1, Township 9 - White
   Fannie - female, age 5

Robbins, G.A. - Range 1, Township 9 - White
   E.T. - female, age 16　　　　　　 T.A. - female, age 7
   Columbus - male, age 14　　　　　 Walter - male, age 5
   M.B. - female, age 11

Robbins, G.W. - Range 1, Township 8 - White
   Katie - female, age 13　　　　　　Winnford - female, age 8
   Bettie - female, age 11　　　　　 Minnie - female, age 6

Robbins, J.A. - Guardian - Range 4, Township 8 - White
   Brazile, Robt - male, age 12　　　Brazile, Lizzie - female, age 10
   Brazile, Ada - female, age 16　　 Brazile, Maggie - female, age 8

Robbins, M.A. - Range 1, Township 9 - White
   Oma - female, age 10　　　　　　　Julia - female, age 5

Robbins, N.F. - Range 1, Township 8 - White
   W.W. - male, age 6

Robbins, Thos - Range 1, Township 9 - Colored
   Mattie - female, age 13　　　　　 John - male, age 5
   Olgal - female, age 8

Robbins, W.T. - Range 1, Township 9 - White
   Maud - female, age 15　　　　　　 Ragie - male, age 6
   Oliver - male, age 13　　　　　　 Myrtle - female, age 6
   Monroe - male, age 10

Roberson, Wm - Range 2, Township 9 - Colored
   Nancy - female, age 18　　　　　　Sandy - male, age 10
   Julia - female, age 16　　　　　　Rubin - male, age 8
   Monroe - male, age 14

Roberts, W.M. - Range 4, Township 11 - Colored
   Jno - male, age 12

Robertson, M.J. - Range 1, Township 10 - White
   M.J. - female, age 17

Robinson, Geo - Range 3, Township 9 - Colored
   Vallie - female, age 13   Chas - male, age 10

Robinson, W.M. - Pontotoc - White
   Frank - male, age 10   Lake - male, age 5
   Willie - male, age 8

Robinson, Young - Range 3, Township 8 - Colored
   Sam - male, age 18   Jno - male, age 9
   Mary - female, age 16   Lula - female, age 5
   Jim - male, age 10

Robinson, Ted - Range 3, Township 9 - Colored
   Mary - female, age 15   Ernest - male, age 11
   Sarah - female, age 18

Roebuck, Tobe - Range 3, Townhip 9 - Colored
   Tobe - male, age 12   Sula - female, age 5
   Laura - female, age 7

Rogers, A.A. - Range 2, Towsnhip 10 - White
   Jas - male, age 18   Chas - male, age 12
   Prissie - female, age 14

Rogers, Frank - Rnge 4, Township 9 - White
   Clyde - female, age 7   Honor - male, age 7
   Glen - male, age 5

Rogers, Geo - Range 4, Township 11 - Colored
   Frank - male, age 15   Joe - male, age 8

Rogers, Geo - Range 4, Township 11 - White
   Geo - male, age 17   Babe - male, age 14
   Frank - male, age 16   Sam - male, age 8

Rogers, Geo - Range 4, Township 11 - White
   Frank - male, age 15

Rogers, H.M. - Range 4, Township 11 - White
   Homer - male, age 19

Roye, H.C. - Range 4, Township 11 - White
   E.S. - female, age 18   Vasaline - female, age 9
   Gideon - male, age 17   Jake - male, age 7
   Bulah - female, age 15   Jessee - male, age 5

Rogers, Giles - Range 3, Township 8 - Colored
   Ida - female, age 18   Mollie - female, age 11
   Moses - male, age 16   Mattie - female, age 7
   Sulia - female, age 14

Rogers, J.D. - Range 1, Township 9 - White
   Adolphus - male, age 9   Toy - male, age 6

Rogers, J.F. - Toccopola - White
   Ila - female, age 20   Mollie - female, age 15
   Archer - male, age 18

Rogers, Jake - Range 4, Township 11 - Colored
   Ada - femle, age 15   Anna - female, age 9
   Sarah - female, age 20   Ann - female, age 7
   Wm - male, age 12   Jno - male, age 8

Rogers, Lula - RAnge 3, Township 10 - Colored
   Carry - female, age 16   Jane - female, age 9
   Willie - male, age 12

Rogers, T.N. - Range 1, Township 9 - White
   W.A. - male age 16   Dan - male, age 8
   Ida - female, age 14   Pearl - female, age 7
   Stella - female, age 13   Carson - male, age 5
   A.A. - female, age 10

Rogers, W.F. - Range 2, Township 10 - White
   W.F. - male, age 17   J.J. - male, age 11
   M.V. - female, age 16   J.W. - male, age 9
   S.E. - female, age 14   G.C. - male, age 7
   M.E. - male, age 20

Rogers, W.F. - Range 2, Township 10 - White
   Foster - male, age 6   Lilian - female, age 5

Rooker, John - Range 2, Township 9 - Colored
   Mollie - female, age 17   Wm - male, age 12
   Chas - female, age 17   Cordie - female, age 9
   Geo - male, age 14

Rowan, T.M. - Guardian - Range 4, Township 8 - White
   Rolan, Lou - female, age 16   Rolan, John - male, age 14
   Rolan , Dollie - female, age 15 Rolan, Gardner - male, age 9
   Rolan, Carry - female, age 10

Rowan, T.M. - Range 4, Township 8 - White
   GEo - male, age 17   Fannie - female, age 12
   Harvy - male, age 11   Ethel - female, age 9
   Emma - female, age 16

Rowland, A.J. - Pontotoc - White
   Chas - male, age 16   Mamie - female, age 11
   Richard - male, age 13   Ed - male, age 8

Rowland, Chas - Range 4, Township 9 - Colored
   Lee - male, age 5

Rowland, Chas - Guardian - Range 4, Township 9 - Colored
   Miller, Dan - male, age 19   Miller, Ben - male, age 9
   Miller, Wes - male, age 8   Miller, Cora - female, age 10

Roye, Mrs. H. - Range 3, Township 11 - White
   Lou - female, age 19   Porter - male, age 17

Roye, H.C. - Range 3, Township 11 - White
   E.S. - female, age 18   Vassille - female, age 9
   Gideon - male, age 17   Jno - male, age 7
   Mary - female, age 15   Jessie - female, age 5
   Eula - female, age 13

Roye, Mrs. H. - Range 4, Township 11 - White
   Lula - female, age 19   Lena - female, age 13
   Porter - male, age 17   Verona - female, age 10

Rowzee, J.H. - Pontotoc - White
   Madison - male, age 17   Marion - male, age 8

Rucker, Range 3, Township 9 - Colored
   Lawrence - male, age 10   Will - male, age 6
   Andrew - male, age 8

Rucker, R.T. - Range 1, Township 8 - White
   Frances - female, age 17   Alvetta - female, age 12
   Ollie - female, age 14

Rush, D.J. - Range 4, Township 9 - White
   Allen - male, age 13   Annie - female, age 20
   Luther - male, age 7

Russell, D.F. - Range 4, Township 9 - White
   Lizzie - female, age 6

Russell, J.G. - Range 4, Township 9 - White
   Wallace - male, age 18   Claud - male, age 10
   Etta - female, age 16   Tera - female, age 8
   Andy - male, age 14   Mattie - female, age 6
   Oscar - male, age 12

Russell, J.G. - Guardian - Range 4, Township 9 -White
   Wilder, Lester - male, age 5

Russell, J.G. - Range 1, Township 8 - White
   John - male, age 18   Minnie - female, age 14
   Willie - female, age 16

Russell, H.H. - Range 1, Township 8 - White
   George - male, age 20   Rindale - female, age 13
   Maggie - female, age 16   Ida - female, age 8

Russell, Jno. A. - Range 4, Township 9 - White
   C.C. - female, age 19   Millie - female, age 15
   Frances - female, age 17   Hattie - female, age 5

Russell, M.I. - Range 3, Township 11 - White
   Lena - female, age 13   Luther - male, age 7
   Ethel - female, age 9   Houston - male, age 5

Russell, M.I. - Range 4, Township 11 - White
   Vallie - female, age 13   Luther - male, age 7
   Ethel - female, age 9   Houston - male, age 5

Russell, M.S. - Range 3, Township 11 - White
   T.A. - female, age 15   R.W. - male, age 9

Russell, P.H. - Range 4, Township 9 - White
   Maud - female, age 6

Russell, W.V. - Range 1, Township 9 - White
   Beulah - female, age 7

Rutledge, Ben - Range 4, Township 10 - Colored
   Gertrude - female, age 9   Frances - female, age 5
   Addie - female, age 7

Rutledge, J.H. - Troy - White
   Mallie - female, age 19   Cordie - female, age 12
   Anna - female, age 17   Daisy - female, age 8
   Bulah - female, age 15   Alias - male, age 10

Rutledge, J.M. - Range 4, Township 11 - White
    Elvira - female, age 8   Jno - male, age 5
    Madison - male, age 6

Rutledge, M.A. - Range 1, Township 9 - White
    James - male, age 17   Jane - female, age 12
    Fannie - female, age 15   Alack - male, age 10

Rutledge, S.H. - Range 4, Township 11 - White
    Flora - female, age 14   Chas - male, age 7
    Jno - male, age 11   Elzy - male, age 6
    Nannie - female, age 9

Salmon, S.A. - Range 2, Township 10 - White
    Coleman - male, age 13   Elmon - male, age 7
    Augusta - female, age 11   Leona - female, age 5

Sandus, H.R. - Range 2, Township 10 - White
    Nelson - male, age 19   Minnie - female, age 9
    Lee - male, age 17   Robt - male, age 7
    Will - male, age 15

Sanders, H.W. - Range 2, Township 10 - White
    Ruth - female, age 11

Sanders, Mrs. N.E. - Range 4, Township 9 - White
    Thos - male, age 19   Susie - female, age 12
    Willie - male, age 15

Sanders, W.S. - Range 1, Township 9 - White
    John - male, age 16   Luster - male, age 5
    Sallie - female, age 10

Sanley, Wm - Range 3, Township 10 - Colored
    Bettie - female, age 18   Wm - male, age 10

Sanly, Rich'd - Range 3, Township 10 - Colored
    Sam - male, age 20   Bibbie - female, age 10
    Lillie - female, age 17   Frank - male, age 8
    James - male, age 15   Lee - male, age 7
    Jno - male, age 13   Ada - female, age 5

Sansing, D.G. - Range 2, Township 11 - White
    Clyde - male, age 11   Ella - female, age 7
    N.V. - female, age 9

Sansing, G.D. - Range 3, Township 11 - White
    Clyde -female, age 13   Ellis - male, age 9
    Vara - female, age 10   Byron - male, age 7

Sappington, R.A. - Range 4, Township 10 - White
    Josie - female, age 20   Lula - female, age 12
    Moses - male, age 16   Jane - female, age 10
    Geo - male, age 18

Sappington, R.L. - Range 4, Township 10 - White
    Maudie - female, age 5

Sappington, Mrs. Bettie - Range 4, Township 9 - White
    Eugene - male, age 18   Wesley - male, age 14

Sappington, P.B. - Range 4, Township 9 - White
   Clavelle - female, age 5

Satterwhite, Nelson - Range 4, Township 8 - Colored
   Calom - male, age 18   Bettie - female, age 12
   Fletcher - male, age 13   Lucy - female, age 10

Satterwhite, S. - Range 4, Township 8 - Colored
   Dollie - female, age 6

Savely, J.W. - Range 3, Township 11 - White
   Chas - male, age 18   Ellen - female, age 8
   Maggie - female, age 17   Frank - male, age 15
   Andrew - male, age 12   Scott - male, age 7
   Susie - female, age 11   Virgie - female, age 5

Savely, R.E. - Guardian - Range 3, Township 11 - White
   Beeson, Bettie - female, age 20   Beeson, Emma - female, age 11
   Beeson, Eula - female, age 18   Beeson, Robt - male, age 9
   Beeson, James - male, age 17   Beeson, Malinda - female, age 6
   Beeson, Anna - female, age 13

Scott, Aaron - Range 3, Township 9 - Colored
   Ida - female, age 15   Hannah - female, age 9

Scott, John - Range 3, Township 9 - Colored
   Willie - male, age 7   Sam - male, age 5

Scott, P.C. - Range 3, Township 9 - Colored
   Frank - male, age 11   Annie - female, age 15
   Rich'd - male, age 10   Laura - female, age 7

Scott, Sim - Range 3, Township 10 - Colored
   Tode - female, age 7

Scott, Tom - Range 3, Township 8 - Colored
   Ed - male, age 16   Will - male, age 12
   Zella - female, age 15   Jno - male, age 9

Scott, Yancy - Range 3, Township 9 - Colored
   Florence - female, age 13   Sallie - female, age 7
   Emma - female, age 9

Scruggs, L.T. - Range 4, Township 8 - White
   Mary - female, age 18   Bell - female, age 12

Seale, G.R. - Range 1, Township 9 - White
   Estelle - female, age 14

Seale, Mrs. A.M. - Troy - White
   Nannie - female, age 19   Ben - male, age 13
   Jack - male, age 17   Jessee - male, age 8

Seale, W.A. - Range 2, Township 9 - White
   M.A. - female, age 14   Tishey - female, age 7
   Willie - female, age 11

Seale, W.H. - Range 4, Township 10 - White
   Lawrence - male, age 20   Hester - female, age 13
   Florence - female, age 17   Ira - male, age 11
   Modenia - female, age 15

Seale, W.M. - Range 1, Township 9 - White
   Sippie - female, age 6   Vandy - male, age 5

Segars, E.C. - Range 2, Township 11 - White
   Mattie - female, age 5

Setzler, G.M. - Range 2, Township 9 - White
   Lula - female, age 5

Sewell, J.A. - Range 4, Township 11 - White
   Mary - female, age 19   Robt - male, age 11
   Elizabeth - female, age 16   Addie - female, age 6
   Lillie - female, age 14

Sewell, Sam - Range 3, Township 11 - White
   Nettie - female, age 10   Seward - male, age 6
   Walter - male, age 9

Shackleford, Thad - Range 3, Township 9 - Colored
   Lizzie - female, age 9   Augusta - male, age 5

Shannon, T.M. - Range 3, Township 10 - White
   Carrie - female, age 15

Shannon, D. - Range 4, Township 11 - Colored
   Oscar - male, age 15   Ella - female, age 9
   Chester - male, age 11   Alice - female, age 5

Shannon, Rolly - Range 3, Township 10 - Colored
   Lena - female, age 12   Andrew - male, age 8
   Ella - female, age 10   Mattie - female, age 6

Shannon, W.C. - Troy - White
   Cora - female, age 16   Thad - male, age 10
   Earle - female, age 13   Jourguine - male, age 7

Sharp, E.G. - Toccopola - White
   Colie - female, age 13   Zora - female, age 8
   Zula - female, age 11   Qubelle - female, age 6

Sharp, W.H. - Toccopola - White
   Dave - male, age 16   Effie - female, age 10
   Maudie - female, age 14   Jodie - female, age 7

Short, J.T. - Toccopola - White
   E.L. - male, age 17   Lewis - male, age 10
   J.T. - male, age 13   Jno - male, age 8

Shelton, D.G. - Range 4, Township 8 - White
   Edgar - male, age 19   Leonard - male, age 14
   Ernest - male, age 17

Shelton, D.G. - Guardian - Range 4, Township 8 - White
   McCraw, Mollie - female, age 17   McCraw, Burrah - male, age 6

Shempert, Sallie - Range 3, Township 10 - White
   Buster - male, age 17   Maggie - female, age 8

Shepard, R.G. - Range 4, Township 9 - White
   Claud - male, age 8   Lena - female, age 5

Shettles, G.W. - Range 4, Township 9 - White
   Eddie - male, age 19   Jno - male, age 15
   Polly - female, age 17

Shirley, N.L. - Rnge 1, Township 9 - White
   Nora - female, age 18   Julia - female, age 13
   Robt - male, age 16   J.P. - male, age 8

Shoemaker, Sarah - Range 2, Township 9 - White
   Jas - male, age 17   Burrell - male, age 7
   Charley - male, age 13

Shoemaker, T.H. - Range 1, Township 9 - White
   Russell - male, age 11   Susie - female, age 9

Shettles, D.P. - Range 2, Township 9 - White
   Sallie - female, age 19   Oma - female, age 7

Short, W.E. - Range 1, Township 8 - White
   Mattie - female, age 14   Loyd - male, age 7
   Lark - male, age 10   Bucker - male, age 7

Shirley, G.W. - Range 4, Township 9 - White
   Mary - female, age 17   Mattie - female, age 8
   Barney - male, age 11

Shields, R.B. - Range 3, Township 10 - White
   Georgia - female, age 9   Joe - male, age 7

Simmons, D. - Range 4, Township 10 - Colored
   Epsie - female, age 15   Tabitha - female, age 7

Simmons, Dave - Range 4, Township 11 - Colored
   Peyton - male, age 16   Robt - male, age 11
   Dora - female, age 14   Irene - female, age 8
   Boston - male, age 13   Johnson, Jim - male, age 15

Simmons, J.B. - Range 1, Township 9 - White
   Maggie - female, age 5

Simmons, G.R. - Range 4, Township 9 - White
   Walter - male, age 6

Simmons, J.A. - Range 4, Township 9 - White
   Margaret - female, age 7   Joshua - male, age 7

Simmons, J.J. - Range 1, Township 10 - White
   Chas - male, age 20

Simmons, Jas - Range 3, Township 11 - Colored
   Walter - male, age 14   Jeff - male, age 11

Simmons, J.W. - Guardian - Range 3, Township 9 - White
   Caldwell, Lizzie - femlae, age 18

Simmons, Mrs. M.A. - Range 4, Township 10 - White
   Geo - male, age 19   Mary - female, age 10
   Jno - male, age 14

Simmons, Newt - Range 3, Township 10 - Colored
   Susie - female, age 8   Lou - female, age 5

Simmons, Ophelia - Range 4, Township 10 - Colored
   Jessee - male, age 9   Cordie - female, age 6
   Lon - male, age 8

Simmons, W.M., Sr. - Range 4, Township 9 - White
   Lula - female, age 13   Walter - male, age 10
   Pristina - female, age 11

Simons, A.B. - Range 4, Township 10 - White
   Emma - female, age 17   Joe - male, age 9
   Allerd - male, age 14   Blaine - female, age 6
   Belle - female, age 12

Sims, W.B. - Range 4, Township 9 - White
   Jno - male, age 9   Rosa - female, age 6

Simon, Alf - Range, Township 8 - Colored
   Annie - female, age 6

Simpson, G.W. - Range 2, Township 9 - White
   Rose - female, age 18   James - male, age 9
   Etta - female, age 12   Willie - female, age 7

Simpson, John - Range 1, Township 8 - White
   Annie - female, age 15

Singleton, Wm - Range 1, Township 11 - White
   Plenie - female, age 17   Jno - male, age 8
   Lem - male, age 11

Skinner, R.L. - Range 1, Township 10 - White
   Jessee - male, age 18   Bettie - female, age 5
   Bulah - female, age 15

Slaughter, H.P. - Range 1, Township 9 - White
   Rester - male, age 10

Slaughter, J.G. - Range 1, Township 9 - White
   Wm - male, age 18   Martha - female, age 8
   Tom - male, age 19   David - male, age 6
   Annie - female, age 14   Bennie - male, age 5
   Jennie - female, age 11

Slaughter, J.T. - Range 1, Township 9 - White
   Charlie - male, age 16   Lillie - female, age 10
   Florence - female, age 14   Bettie - female, age 8
   Needon - male, age 12

Slaughter, R.G. - Range 1, Township 9 - White
   Jennie - female, age 9   Ike - male, age 5
   David - male, age 7

Sledge, C.A. - Range 1, Township 10 - White
   Winnie - female, age 12   Lena - female, age 8
   Edna - female, age 0   Doce - female, age 5

Sledge, C.F. - Range 1, Township 10 - White
   Nancy - female, age 15   Perry, male, age 10
   Emma - female, age 14

Sledge, E.M. - Range 1, Township 9 - White
   Sallie - female, age 16

Sledge, H.B. - Range 1, Township 10 - White
   Ellis - male, age 9   Jno - male, age 7

Sledge, M.D. - Range 1, Township 9 - White
   Ez - male, age 10   M.B. - female, age 7

Sledge, M.P. - Range 1, Township 10 - White
   Calvin - male, age 7   Livington - male, age 5

Sledge, T.F. - Range 1, Township 9 - White
   Mazie - female, age 16

Sloan, M. - Guardian - Range 3, Township 11 - Colored
   Herd, Thos - male, age 18   Herd, Hannah - female, age 7
   Herd, Peter - male, age 16

Smith, Alex - Range 4, Township 9 - Colored
   Vina - female, age 18   Mary - female, age 19
   Robt - male, age 12

Smith, Alice - Range 2, Township 11 - Colored
   Alex - male, age 18   Collums, Jno - male, age 19
   Andrew - male, age 10   Collums, Sam - male, age 16
   Fester - male, age 6   Duke, Thos - male, age 14
   Lou - female, age 5

Smith, Frank - Range 2, Township 9 - Colored
   Frank - male, age 18   Susie - female, age 14
   Will - male, age 17   Chas - male, age 11

Smith, G.W. - Range 4, Townhip 11 - White
   Elizabeth - female, age 17   Rinda - female, age 5
   Martha - female, age 9

Smith, J.B. - Range 1, Township 9 - White
   Hattie - female, age 13   Bertice - female, age 7
   Jane - female, age 10   Lula - female, age 5

Smith, J.B. - Range 1, Township 9 - White
   Mattie - female, age 12   John - male, age 8
   Elma - female, age 10   Joe - male, age 6

Smith, J.W. - Range 2, Township 11 - White
   Rush - male, age 9   Word - male, age 7

Smith, Jas - Range 3, Township 9 - White
   Mary - female, age 16   Walter - male, age 12
   Bulah - female, age 14

Smith, L.M. - Range 3, Township 9 - White
   Maggie - female, age 14   Willis - male, age 6
   Carry - female, age 10

Smith, Mrs. Lizzie - Range 4, Township 10 - White
   Wiley - male, age 16   Lela - female, age 10
   Frank - male, age 14   Hattie - female, age 8
   Lou - female, age 12

Smith, Mrs. M.L. - Range 1, Township 8 - White
   J.B. - male, age 18   P.E. - male, age 14
   J.P. - male, age 15

Smith, M.M. - Range 3, Township 8 - White
   Raymon - male, age 19   Lillie - female, age 9
   Norton - male, age 10

Smith, Marn - Guardian - Range 2, Township 11 - White
   Owen, Addie - female, age 15   Owen, Meloin - male, age 12
   Owen, Jno - male, age 14

Smith, N.B. - Range 1, Township 9 - White
   Willie - male, age 11   Eddie - male, age 5
   Sylvia - female, age 8

Smith, Nip - Range 1, Township 10 - White
   Eva - female, age 15   Jno - male, age 10
   Jane - female, age 13

Smith, Robt - Range 2, Township 9 - Colored
   Sarah - female, age 12   Lewis - male, age 10

Smith, W.M. - Range 4, Township 8 - White
   Raymon - male, age 19   Lillie - female, age 9
   Nora - female, age 13

Smith, W.W. - Range 2, Township 9 - White
   Fred - male, age 15   Jessee - male, age 5
   Zula - female, age 14

Smitherman, J. - Range 2, Township 9 - White
   Hugh - male, age 9   Lou - female, age 5
   Maudie - female, age 7

Smitherman, J.W. - Range 1, Township 10 - White
   Ida - female, age 16   Eva - female, age 11

Smitherman, Jno - Range 1, Township 9 - White
   Wm - male, age 18   Mary - female, age 12
   Lena - female, age 14

Smitherman, S.N. - Range 4, Township 9 - White
   Lou - female, age 16   Ernest - male, age 5
   Jessie - female, age 19

Sneed, A.B. - Range 1, Township 9 - White
   Bulah - female, age 13   Madie - female, age 9
   James - male, age 11   Helen - female, age 7

Sneed, A.L. - Range 1, Township 8 - White
   N.G. - female, age 16   Julia - female, age 8
   James - male, age 13   Camelia - female, age 6
   Vela - female, age 11

Sneed, J.L. - Range 1, Township 8 - White
   Oscar - male, age 7   Montee - female, age 5

Sneed, J.L. - Guardian - Range 1, Township 8 - White
   Robbins, Isaac - male, age 8

Snider, Nannie - Range 1, Township 11 - White
   Nellie - female, age 7   Rachael - female, age 5

Souter, J.T. - Pontotoc, - White
   Lewis - male, age 10   Robt - male, age 6
   Mary - female, age 8

Souter, James - Range 2, Township 10 - Colored
   Frances - female, age 5

Souter, Jas - Range 2, Township 9 - Colored
   Frank - male, age 15   Walter - male, age 10
   Sleeter - male, age 12   Mary - female, age 6

Southern, Dan - Range 4, Township 11 - Colored
   Sareph - female, age 14   Lillie - female, age 12

Spaks, Susie - Range 3, Township 9 - White
   Virgil - male, age 15   Eddie - female, age 8

Sparks, Mrs. Susan - Range 3, Township 8 - White
   Narcissa - female, age 19   Eddie - male, age 14
   Virgia - female, age 16

Spearman, Bill - Range 4, Township 8 - Colored
   Percilla - female, age 9   Lem - male, age 5
   Nannie - female, age 7

Spearman, Geo - Range 4, Township 9 - Colored
   Zelia - female, age 15   Willie - male, age 12
   Henry - male, age 18   Burrell - male, age 5

Spears, A.J. - Range 1, Township 9 - White
   Josie - female, age 10   Leona - female, age 5
   Jane - female, age 7

Spencer, A.H. - Range 3, Township 10 - White
   Robt - male, age 20   Frank - male, age 13
   Walter - male, age 18   Emory - male, age 9
   Sidney - male, age 16   Mary - female, age 6

Spencer, A.W.C. - Range 1, Township 9 - White
   Annie - female, age 18   Julia - female, age 14

Spencer, W.R. - Range 3, Township 8 - White
   George - male, age 17

Springer, D. - Range 4, Township 11 - White
   Florida - female, age 18   Myrtie - female, age 11
   Ed - male, age 13   Lula - female, age 8

Springer, J.L. - Range 4, Township 9 - White
   Lucy - female, age 20   Willie - female, age 11
   Katie - female, age 18   Octava - female, age 9
   Jeanette - female, age 13

Stafford, Katie - Range 2, Township 11 - White
   Will - male, age 17

Stafford, Kittie - Range 3, Township 11 - White
   Wm - male, age 17

Staggers, J.H. - Range 4, Township 11 - White
   Sam - male, age 11   Willie - male, age 9
   Laura - female, age 10   Mattie - female, age 6

Stanford, H.C. - Pontotoc - White
   Alma - female, age 18

Stanford, J.W. - Range 4, Township 11 - White
   Carrie - female, age 15   Cora - female, age 7
   Pearl - female, age 11

Stark, T.T. - Range 3, Township 8 - White
   Tom - male, age 20   Rufus - male, age 12
   Sallie - female, age 18   Fannie - female, age 8

Starks, Collie - Range 3, Township 10 - Colored
   Cenie - female, age 19   Chas - male, age 14
   Joe - male, age 16   Jane - female, age 12

Starks, Tennie - Pontotoc - Colored
   Jessie - female, age 12   Jane - female, age 6
   Nood - male, age 14

Staten, E. - Range 3, Township 11 - White
   Minnie - female, age 18

Staten, M.F. - Range 3, Township 11 - White
   Susie - female, age 18   Davy - male, age 8
   Isabella - female, age 13   Lou - female, age 5
   Walter - male, age 10

Staten - Mrs. L.J. - Range 3, Township 11 - White
   Lisle - male, age 18

Staten, Tobe - Range 1, Townsip 11 - White
   Jim - male, age 8   Arthur - male, age 6

Staten, Wm - Range 4, Township 10 - White
   Myrtle - female, age 11   Lula - female, age 5
   Ed - male, age 7

Steele, M.P. - Range 1, Township 11 - White
   Monroe - male, age 9   Ara - female, age 5
   Isam - male, age 7

Steele, W.A.J. - Guardian - Range 1, Township 11 - White
   Roebuck, Dillard - male, age 13   Roebuck, Cynthia - female, age 7
   Roebuck, Artway - male, age 11   Roebuck, Manie - female, age 5
   Roebuck, Morgan - male, age 9

Stegall, C.W. - Range 4, Township 11 - White
   J.S. - male, age 20   Dora - female, age 10
   C.W. - male, age 16   Bulah - female, age 8
   J.A. - male, age 14

Stegall, J.G. - Rnge 4, Township 11 - White
   Dolly - female, age 19   Jerry - male, age 11
   Jno - male, age 17   Annie - female, age 13

Stegall, J.M. - Range 3, Township 10 - White
   Jas - male, age 16   Geo - male, age 19

Stegall, M.B. - Range 4, Township 11 - White
   Willie - male, age 14   Edward - male, age 7
   Luther - male, age 9   Jessie - female, age 5

Stegall, R.C. - Range 4, Township 10 - White
   A.J. - male, age 5

Stegall, T.M. - Range 3, Township 9 - White
   Chas - female, age 5

Stepp, S.W. - Range 4, Township 10 - White
   L.E. - male, age 18   M.L. - female, age 12
   M.E. - female, age 15   Mary - female, age 9

Stepp, Wm - Range 3, Township 9 - White
   Lou - female, age 19   Andrew - male, age 5
   Ulyss - male, age 17

Stevens, D.B. - Range 4, Township 10 - White
   Robt - male, age 9   Rena - female, age 6
   Jetta - male, age 8

Stevens, E.D. - Range 2, Township 9 - White
   Myrtie - female, age 13   Laura - female, age 8
   Willie - male, age 11   Pearl - female, age 7
   Ise - female, age 9   Grover - male, age 5

Stevens, Gus - Range 3, Township 9 - Colored
   Joe - male, age 18   Susie - female, age 6
   Park, male, age 15   Fred - male, age 6
   Quitman - male, age 10   Laura - female, age 16
   Ivy - male, age 8

Stevens, J.M. - Range 4, Township 8 - White
   Hardy - male, age 10   Lizzie - female, age 5

Stevens, Perry - Range 3, Township 9 - Colored
   Chas - male, age 10   Mary - female, age 8

Stewart, B.W. - Troy - White
   Jessie - female, age 15

Stewart, J.K. - Range 4, Township 11 - White
   Zack - male, age 18   Kelly - male, age 10
   Alma - female, age 17   Staten - male, age 7
   Leland - male age 16   Preston - male age 5
   Estelle - female, age 12

Stewart, J.M. - Range 1, Township 10 - White
   Emily - female, age 18   Flora - female, age 12
   Jabus - male, age 14   Frank - male, age 7

Stewart, J.R. - Range 1, Township 10 - White
   Atta - female, age 16   Gena - female, age 10
   Augustus - male, age 14   Lizzie - female, age 7
   Ira - female, age 12

Stewart, Oliver - Range 3, Township 11 - Colored
   Wm - male, age 18   Luvada - female, age 10
   Lorenzo - male, age 16   Annie - female, age 8
   Jessee - male, age 13   Ida - female, age 7

Stewart, Oliver - Range 3, Township 10 - Colored
   Wm - male, age 18   Anna - female, age 8
   Lorenzo - male, age 16   Ada - female, age 7
   Jessee - male, age 13   Jane - female, age 6
   Lou - female, age 10

Stewart, P.S. - Range 3, Township 11 - Colored
   Robt - male, age 18   Sam - male age 16

Stewart, R.G. - Rnge 3, Townhip 11 - White
   Thos - male, age 13   Anna - female, age 7

Stewart, R.T. - Range 4, Township 10 - Colored
   Tom - male, age 17   Jet - male, age 12
   Scrap - male, age 15   Effort - male, age 6

Stewart, S.S. - Range 1, Township 11 - White
    Ada - female, age 12   Hershel - male, age 6
    Loyce - male, age 8

Stewart, Wm - Range 3, Township 11 - Colored
    Jno - male age 18   Mary - female, age 12
    Wm - male, age 16   Myrtle - female, age 11
    Sarah - female, age 13   Maggie - female, age 6

Strange, Mrs. M.A. - Range 4, Township 11 - White
    Robt - male, age 17   Susan - female, age 11
    Meddie - female, age 14

Stubbs, Francis - Range 4, Township 11 - Colored
    Maria - female, age 13   Lee - male, age 7
    Lizzie - female, age 10   Oliver - male, age 5

Suddoth, J.M. - Range 4, Township 9 - White
    Joe - male, age 10   Jno - male age 6
    Vivian - female, age 9

Suddoth, Mrs. N.D. - Range 3, Township 10 - White
    May - female, age 9   Thursa - female, age 7

Suddoth, W.O. - Range 4, Township 10 - White
    Willie - male, age 17   Robt - male, age 14

Suggs, B.H. - Range 4, Township 8 - White
    Eddie - male, age 12

Suraeyor, Wesly - Range 3, Township 10 - Colored
    Jno - male, age 6

Surrett, B.C. - Range 4, Township 11 - White
    Mary - female, age 20   Anna - female, age 11
    W.T. - male, age 17   Mattie - female, age 8
    Ella - female, age 15   Ed - male, age 6
    Nannie - female, age 13

Surrett, D.C. - Range 4, Township 11 - White
    S.P. - male, age 10   Minnie - female, age 5
    J.S. - male, age 8

Swaim, J.W. - Range 1, Township 10 - White
    Quitman - male, age 19   Heley - male, age 11
    Ollie - female, age 17   Berry - male, age 8
    Laura - female, age 15   Onie - female, age 5
    Dora - female, age 13

Swindoll, C.R. - Range 4, Township 9 - White
    Sarah - female, age 15   Willie - male, age 14

Swindoll, J.S. - Range 4, Township 9 - White
    Maggie - female, age 6

Swords, A.J. - Range 2, Township 9 - White
    Mattie - female, age 18   Alia - female, age 6
    Annie - female, age 14

Sykes, J.L. - Range 1, Township 11 - White
    Jas - male, age 10   Chas - male, age 7
    Georgia - female, age 9

Tallant, Frank - Range 1, Township 10 - White
   Lige - male, age 12　　　　　　　　Luther - male, age 8
   Ed - male, age 10　　　　　　　　　Elma - female, age 6

Tallant, J.D. - Range 1, Township 10 - White
   Jas - male, age 15

Tankersly, Rebecca - Toccopola - Colored
   B. - male, age 12　　　　　　　　　Lewis - male, age 8
   Mat - male, age 10　　　　　　　　Dickerson, Ed - male, age 18

Tarrant, J.M. - Range 2, Township 10 - White
   A.C. - male, age 12　　　　　　　　D.S. - male, age 8
   A.L. - male, age 10　　　　　　　　Alvin - male, age 5

Tate, H.B. - Range 3, Township 10 - White
   A.A. - male, age 19　　　　　　　　Robt - male, age 13
   Fed - male, age 14　　　　　　　　Virgie - female, age 5

Taylor, J.M.G. - Range 1, Township 11 - White
   Rachael - female, age 19　　　　　　Ora - female, age 10
   Annie - female, age 12

Taylor, John - Range 3, Township 9 - White
   Willie - male, age 12

Taylor, J.M.G. - Guardian - Range 1, Township 11 - White
   Palmer, Jno - male, age 19

Tedford, B.J. - Range 1, Township 11 - White
   Clara - female, age 14　　　　　　　Russell - male, age 7
   Bonnie - female, age 10　　　　　　Jno - male, age 5

Terrell, Mrs. F.E. - Range 1, Township 10 - White
   Wm - male, age 18　　　　　　　　Laura - female, age 12
   Lawrence - male, age 14　　　　　　Emma - female, age 10

Terrell, F.M. - Range 2, Township 8 - White
   Addie - female, age 18　　　　　　　Ruth - female, age 6
   Nixie - female, age 15　　　　　　　Jas - male, age 19
   Flora - female, age 11　　　　　　　Wm - male, age 10
   F.M. - male, age 9　　　　　　　　Louie - female, age 14

Terrell, J.F. - Range 2, Township 8 - White
   Addie - female, age 11　　　　　　　Robt - male, age 18
   Clay - male, age 5　　　　　　　　Tom - male, age 12
   Jno - male, age 18　　　　　　　　Maggie - female, age 7

Tetor, W.J. - Range 4, Township 9 - White
   Alma - female, age 12　　　　　　　Lizzie - female, age 8
   Walter - male, age 10

Thaxton, M.C. - Range 1, Township 9 - White
   C.L. - male, age 13　　　　　　　　L.D. - male, age 10
   L.N. - male, age 11　　　　　　　　M. - female, age 8

Thomas, Frank - Range 2, Township 9 - Colored
   Frank - male, age 20　　　　　　　Wm - male, age 13
   Will - male, age 19　　　　　　　　Emma - female, age 6

Thomas, Dan'l - Range 4, Township 9 - Colored
   Jno - male, age 17　　　　　　　　Jim - male, age 12

Thomason, Mrs. M.E. - Pontotoc - White
   Willie - male, age 17

Thompson, B.H. - Pontotoc - White
   Luther - male, age 8

Thompson, Ben - Range 3, Township 11 - Colored
   Jeff - male, age 18   Fannie - female, age 10
   Sue - female, age 17   Ben - male, age 8
   Walter - male, age 12   Willie - male, age 6

Thompson, Chas - Range 4, Township 11 - Colored
   Lela - female, age 8   Edwards, Ben - male, age 13
   Sam - male, age 6

Thompson, Henry - Range 4, Township 9 - White
   Etta - female, age 19   Chas - male, age 10
   Hybernia - female, age 16   Frances - female, age 7
   Sallie - female, age 13   Luther - male, age 5

Thompson, T.W. - Range 4, Township 9 - White
   Sallie - female, age 10   Lula - female, age 8

Thompson, Wm - Range 3, Township 11 - Colored
   Willie - male, age 15   Nannie - female, age 6
   Burt - male, age 12

Thornton, Frank, Sr. - Range 1, Township 9 - White
   James - male, age 15   Maggie - female, age 5
   John - male, age 9

Thornton, J.M. - Pontotoc - White
   Hattie - female, age 20   Jno - male, age 12
   Bettie - female, age 15

Thornton, W.C. - Range 1, Township 9 - White
   John - male, age 18   Ada - female, age 8
   Cordie - female, age 14   Lela - female, age 6
   Elmo - male, age 9

Tindall, Mrs. L. - Range 1, Township 11 - White
   Neely - female, age 19   Dora - female, age 14
   Tuley - female, age 17

Tindall, Mrs. L. - Guardian - Range 1, Township 11 - White
   Purdon, J.F. - male, age 19   Purdon, L.E. - female, age 20

Todd, J.D. - Range 1, Towsnhip 9 - White
   Cora - female, age 8   Chester - male, age 6

Todd, J.H. - Range 1, Township 8 - White
   Sarah - female, age 14   Columbus - male, age 8
   N.L. - male, age 12   Minnie - female, age 6
   Emma - female, age 10   Ida - female, age 5

Todd, J.L. - Guardian - Range 1, Township 9 - White
   Johnson, Robt - male, age 9

Todd, J.T. - Range 1, Township 8 - White
   Nancy - female, age 18   Monroe - male, age 9
   Robt - male, age 13   Ada - female, age 5
   Dave - male, age 11

Todd, Mrs. A.M. - Pontotoc - White
   W.S. - male, age 18   L.C. - female, age 15

Trott, Jeff - Range 3, Township 9 - Colored
   Henry - male, age 17   Fannie - female, age 10
   Jno - male, age 12

Tubbs, Henry - Range 4, Township 11 - Colored
   Commodore - male, age 13   Maggie - female, age 12

Tucker, A.W. - Range 1, Township 11 - White
   John - male, age 18   Conzada - female, age 11
   Sam - male, age 16   Alf - male, age 8
   Georgia - female, age 13

Tucker, S.J. - Range 3, Township 8 - White
   Addie - female, age 18   Egbert - male, age 15

Tully, H.M. - Range 4, Township 10 - White
   Mary - female, age 16   Hugh - male, age 12
   Susie - female, age 14

Tunnell, J.T. - Range 4, Township 11 - White
   Will - male, age 11   Bettie - female, age 7
   Dave - male, age 8   Toy - male, age 5

Turner, E.C. - Range 1, Township 10 - White
   Minnie - female, age 12   Elisha - male, age 7

Turner, E.T. - Range 1, Township 11 - White
   Dalton - male, age 9   May - female, age 5

Turner, G.W. - Range 1, Township 11 - White
   Chester - male, age 15   Geo - male, age 9
   Etta - female, age 13   Carrie - female, age 6
   Ada - female, age 11

Tutor, A.N.H. - Range 1, Township 10 - White
   Ida - female, age 8   Jno - male, age 5

Tutor, D.H. - Range 1, Township 10 - White
   Lena - female, age 17   Jas - male, age 14
   Lucy - female, age 15   Daniel - male, age 9

Tutor, H.B. - Range 1, Township 10 - White
   Ollie - female, age 12   Cora - female, age 8

Tutor, H.D. - Range 1, Township 11 - White
   Ella - female, age 19   Jas - male, age 14
   Qulla - female, age 16   Labors - male, age 16

Tutor, J. - Range 1, Township 10 - White
   Lonnie - male, age 19   Walter - male, age 10
   Richard - male, age 16   Ida - female, age 8

Tutor, J.D. - Range 1, Township 11 - White
   Mary - female, age 20   Mamon - male, age 11
   Wm - male, age 14   Alex - male, age 9
   Marion - male, age 11   Jno - male, age 7

Tutor, J.W. - Range 1, Township 10 - White
   Viley - female, age 15   Dolphus - male, age 7
   Aggie - female, age 13   Posey - male, age 6
   Sid - male, age 10

Tutor, Joe - Range 1, Township 10 - White
   Andy - male, age 12
   Silas - male, age 10
   Lizzie - female, age 6

Tutor, R.H. - Range 1, Township 10 - White
   Bazella - female, age 20
   Viola - female, age 20
   Bulah - female, age 18
   Arnses - female, age 16
   Lela - female, age 11
   Alice - female, age 10

Tutor, R.O. - Range 1, Township 11 - White
   Callie - female, age 16
   Augusta - male, age 14
   Jas - male, age 12

Tutor, Tom - Range 1, Township 10 - White
   Wm - male, age 19
   Parlee - female, age 17
   Della - female, age 17
   Wyatt - male, age 15
   Dovie - female, age 6

Tutor, Tom - Guardian - Range 1, Township 10 - White
   Buchillon, Henry - male, age 18

Tutor, W.B. - Range 1, Township 10 - White
   Mazie - female, age 10

Tutor, W.H. - Range 1, Township 10 - White
   Bradford - male, age 19
   Pimpton - male, age 18
   Archie - male, age 16
   Arley - female, age 9
   Annie - female, age 7
   Marion - male, age 5

Tutor, W.H. - Range 1, Township 10 - White
   Archie - male, age 17

Tutor, W.F. - Range 1, Township 10 - White
   Charles - male, age 12
   Amos - male, age 10
   Alice - female, age 8

Underwood, W.Q. - Range 1, Township 11 - White
   Minnie - female, age 18
   Addie - female, age 16
   Helen - female, age 14
   Mattie - female, age 9
   Jas - male, age 6

Unknown Parent or Guardian - Range 4, Township 10 White
   Bryon, Henry - male, age 19
   Pitts, Richard - male, age 18

Unknown Parent or Guardian - Range 4, Township 9 - Colored
   Rucker, Thomas - male, age 5

Unknown Parent or Guardian - Range 4, Township 9 - Colored
   Suggs, Hattie - female, age 17
   Suggs, Jno - male, age 13
   Suggs, Bulah - female, age 5

Unknown Parent or Guardian - Range 4, Township 9 - Colored
   Vickerson, Booker - male, age 14

Vance, Antney - Range 4, Township 11 - Colored
   Ed - male, age 16
   Eugene - male, age 12
   Joe - male, age 8

Vance, Ben - Range 1, Township 9 - White
   Susie - female, age 8

Vandivor, T. - Range 4, Township 9 - White
    Jurrel - male, age 17   Thos - male, age 12
    Maggie - female, age 14   Vivia - female, age 5

Vaughn, J.H. - Range 1, Township 9 - White
    Corra - female, age 8   John - male, age 5
    Linnia - female, age 7

Vaughn, J.H. - Guardian - Range 1, Township 9 - White
    Crawford, Gus - male, age 15

Vaughn, Lewis - Range 2, Township 10 - White
    Tucker - male, age 12   Doke - male, age 10

Vaughn, T.J. - Range 1, Township 9 - White
    Martin - male, age 11   Vera - female, age 6
    Octia - female, age 9

Vaughn, W.C. - Range 2, Township 9 - White
    Richard - male, age 20   Fannie - female, age 11
    Lucy - female, age 18

Vincent, J.A. - Range 1, Township 9 - White
    Lela - female, age 6

Vincent, Lewis - Range 4, Township 9 - White
    Walter - male, age 16   Alma - female, age 9
    Henry - male, age 14   Clarence - male, age 9
    Parlee - female, age 13   Geo - male, age 6

Wagner, W.H. - Range 4, Township 9 - White
    Clyde - female, age 9   Lester - male, age 7

Waite, J.D. - Range 1, Township 8 - White
    Walter - male, age 14   Dolph - male, age 11
    Corra - female, age 13   Hershel - male, age 8
    Julia - female, age 12   Gavie - male, age 6

Waldo, E.J. - Range 2, Township 9 - White
    Henry - male, age 18   Jennie - female, age 10
    Ben - male, age 10   Ida - female, age 8

Waldron, Mrs. S. - Range 1, Township 8 - White
    Joe - male, age 11   Katie - female, age 7

Waldrop, W.F. - Toccopola - White
    Jno - male, age 20   Mary - female, age 17

Waldrop, W.H. - Range 1, Township 8 - White
    Ara - female, age 14   Joe - male, age 10
    James - male, age 12   Myrtis - female, age 8

Walker, A.E. - Range 1, Township 8 - White
    Sam - male, age 19   Alpha - male, age 10
    Minnie - female, age 17   John - male, age 8
    Charley - male, age 15   James - male, age 5
    Odus - male, age 11

Walker, Ben - Range 1, Township 11 - White
    Tom - male, age 7   Lucinda - female, age 5

Walker, Caroline - Pontotoc - White
    Sallie - female, age 12   Julia - female, age 8

Walker, Emma - Pontotoc - Colored
   Clinton - male, age 7   Emma - female, age 5
Walker, Lou - Pontotoc - Colored
   Mary - femle, age 18   Lou - female, age 12
   Ed - male, age 15   Jane - female, age 10
   Jennie - female, age 14
Walker, Lucian - Range 4, Township 8 - Colored
   Sanders - male, age 9   Frances - female, age 5
Walker, T.W. - Range 1, Township 11 - White
   Paradine - female, age 15   Palistine - female, age 13
Walker, W.T. - Range 4, Township 11 - White
   Robt - male, age 5
Walls, A.J. - Range 2, Township 11 - White
   Susie - female, age 8   Virgie - female, age 6
Walls, A.J. - Guardian - Range 1, Township 8 - White
   Boothe, Wm - male, age 15   Boothe, Mary - female, age 8
   Boothe, James - male, age 5
Walls, J.B. - Range 2, Township 11 - White
   Anna - female, age 18   Vallie - male, age 10
   Thos - male, age 16   Andrew - male, age 9
   Jas - male, age 14   Jeff - male, age 7
   Rich'd - male, age 12   Wm - male, age 5
Walls, J.R. - Range 3, Township 11 - White
   Oscar - male, age 18   Willie - male, age 13
   Clay - male, age 16   Lee - male, age 10
   Curt - male, age 14
Walls, Jno - Range 3, Township 11 - White
   Wm - male, age 12   Susie - female, age 9
Walls, Joe - Range 4, Township 11 - White
   Maggie - female, age 7   Mary - female, age 5
Walls, W.P. - Range 3, Township 11 - White
   Sulee - female, age 7   Mary - female, age 6
Ward, A. - Range 1, Township 10 - White
   Geo - male, age 10   Lillie - female, age 6
   Alphaloma - female, age 8
Ward, Geo - Range 4, Township 10 - Colored
   Chas - male, age 20   Susan - female, age 8
   Josie - female, age 17   Luvada - female, age 11
   Henry - male, age 15   Wm - male, age 5
Ward, J.S. - Range 3, Township 11 - White
   Daisy - female, age 12   Joe - male, age 8
Ward, James - Range 2, Township 11 - White
   Daisy - female, age 12   Jessie - female, age 8
Ward, Mrs. W.C. - Range 4, Township 9 - White
   Eddie - male, age 18   Bessie - female, age 12
   Birdie - female, age 15

Ward, W.C. - Range 1, Township 8 - White
    Saloame - female, age 13   James - male, age 7
    Lizzie - female, age 10   Geo - male, age 5

Wardlaw, J.T. - Range 2, Township 10 - White
    Jettie - female, age 15   Annie - female, age 7
    Edgar - male, age 13   Rich'd - male, age 6
    Calvin - male, age 10

Wardlaw, J.T. - Guardian - Range 2, Township 10 - White
    Vance, S. - male, age 10

Ware, Alex - Guardian - Range 3, Township 11 - Colored
    Eubanks, Will - male, age 17   Eubanks, Daisy - female, age 8
    Eubanks, Cal - male, age 15   Eubanks, Rachael - female, age 6
    Eubanks, Emma - female, age 13   Stevens, Ed - male, age 17
    Eubanks, Dock - male, age 12   Stevens, Sallie - Female, age 13
    Eubanks, Prestin - male, age 10

Ware, Berry - Range 4, Township 11 - Colored
    Arthur - male, age 9

Ware, Ellen - Range 3, Township 10 - Colored
    Ida - female, age 18   Jerry - male, age 14
    Arthur - male, age 18   Almore - male, age 12
    Joe - male, age 16   Duke - male, age 9
    Sarah - female, age 15   Blanch - female, age 7

Ware, Ella - Range 3, Township 11 - Colored
    Ida - female, age 21   D.W. - male, age 10
    E.J. - female, age 18   R.L. - male, age 10
    Jerry - male, age 14   A.L. - male, age 8

Ware, J.H. - Guardian - Range 3, Township 9 - Colored
    Rhoda - female, age 17   Harrison - male, age 10
    Thos - male, age 15   Wm - male, age 5

Ware, J.J. - Range 4, Township 11 - Colored
    Caroline - female, age 14   Jas - male, age 8
    Katie - female, age 12   Susan - female, age 5
    Obey - male, age 10

Ware, Jerry - Range 3, Township 11 - Colored
    Sanlen - male, age 17   Arthur - male, age 8
    Mitch - male, age 15   Barber - male, age 5
    Cain - male, age 12

Ware, Mrs. Dan - Range 2, Township 11 - White
    John - male, age 20

Ware, Rhoda - Range 2, Township 9 - Colored
    Ann - female, age 12   Jim - male, age 8
    Sam - male, age 10   Mary - female, age 5

Ware, Sam - Range 4, Township 11 - Colored
    Parlee - female, age 11   Obey - male, age 5
    Nancy - female, age 6   Wheeler, Callie - female, age 15

Ware, W.T. - Range 4, Township 11 - White
    Wm - male, age 19   Jno - male, age 11
    Lemuel - male, age 17   Mary - female, age 9

Ware, Wash - Range 4, Township 11 - Colored
   w.M. - male, age 17   Albert - male age 17
   J.H. - male, age 16   Jas - male, age 10
   A.W. - male, age 14

Warren, A. Range 1, Township 8 - White
   Alf - male, age 16   Joe - male, age 14

Warren, A. - Guardian - Range 1, Township 8 - White
   Mahan, Mart - male, age 9

Warren, D.W. - Range 3, Township 11 - White
   Jno - male, age 11   Fred - male, age 6

Warren, J.H. - Range 1, Township 8 - White
   Wm - male, age 20   Lizzie - female, age 14
   Mary - female, age 18   Lula - female, age 7
   Frances - female, age 17   Montie - female, age 5

Warren, J.H. - Range 3, Township 9 - White
   Thos - male, age 12   Allie - female, age 6
   Nannie - female, age 10

Warren, J.M. - Range 4, Township 9 - White
   Ida - female, age 16   Thos - male, age 11
   Minnie - female, age 15   Jno - male, age 8
   Josie - female, age 13   Robt - male, age 5

Warren, J.P. - Range 1, Township 8 - White
   Roxie - female, age 20   Geo - male, age 13
   James - male, age 18   Harry - male, age 10
   Richard - male, age 16   Ellic - male, age 7

Warren, J.R. - Range 1, Township 8 - White
   James - male, age 16   Homer - male, age 10
   Lonnie - male, age 14   Grover - male, age 7
   Joe - male, age 12   John - male, age 5

Warren, J.R. - Guardian - Range 1, Township 8 - White
   Minnie - female, age 15   Martin - male, age 7
   Dillie - female, age 13   Lizzie - female, age 6
   Cordie - female, age 11   Immer - female, age 5

Warren, J.R. - Range 3, Township 11 - White
   Wm - male, age 20   Emma - female, age 13
   Ludie - female, age 18   Katie - female, age 11
   Jessee - male, age 17   Pike - male, age 9
   Curtis - male, age 15   Jas - male, age 6

Warren, Jno - Range 4, Township 10 - White
   Ollie - female, age 9   Daisy - female, age 6

Warren, T.R. - Range 4, Township 9 - White
   Robt - male, age 15   Emma - female, age 8
   Ila - female, age 12   Myrtie - female, age 5
   Luther - male, age 10

Warren, Z.W. - Range 1, Township 8 - White
   Minnie - female, age 10   Richard - male, age 14

Washington, J.H. - Range 1, Township 11 - White
   J.H. - male, age 19   Marion - male, age 7
   Albert - male, age 14

Washington, J.P. - Range 2, Township 11 - White
   Geo - male, age 10   Elco - male, age 8

Washington, Jno - Guardian - Range 1, Township 11 - White
   Phillips, Elena - female, age 10   Phillips, Egbert - male, age 8

Waters, M.J. - Range 4, Township 11 - White
   Robt - male, age 5

Waters, W.R. - Range 1, Township 8 - White
   Wm - male, age 10   Lizzie - female, age 5
   Mary - female, age 8

Watkins, M.M. - Range 4, Township 9 - White
   Florence - female, age 17

Watts, A.J. - Range 3, Township 9 - White
   Carrie - female, age 18   Mary - female, age 7
   John - male, age 17   Leslie, Ed - male, age 16
   Lawrence - male, age 14   Leslie, Celia - femlae, age 16
   Alma - female, age 12

Watts, D.F. - Range 3, Township 9 - White
   Walter - male, age 15   Mattie - female, age 7
   Wallace - male, age 13   Chas - male, age 5

Watts, Jeff - Range 2, Township 10 - White
   Jas - male, age 18   Ivy - male, age 10
   Barbie - female, age 18   Wesly - male, age 6
   Marion - male, age 16

Watts, Wesly - Range 3, Township 9 - Colored
   Jno - male, age 20   Chas - male, age 12
   Henry - male, age 15   Zepher - female, age 8
   Walter - male, age 16

Waugh, Robt - Range 1, Township 10 - White
   Lou - female, age 20   Mary - female, age 16
   Jno - male, age 18   Robt - male, age 14

Weaver, T.P. - Range 2, Township 10 - White
   Willie - male, age 9   Sam - male, age 5
   Lela - female, age 7

Weatherall, A. - Range 3, Township 9 - Colored
   Eliza - female, age 16   Martha - female, age 8
   Andrew - male, age 10

Weatherall, Adline - Range 3, Township 9 - Colored
   Addie - female, age 10

Weatherall, Ben - Range 3, Township 9 - Colored
   Ben - male, age 17   Jno - male, age 9
   Sanford - male, age 13   Dan - male, age 6
   Ed - male, age 12

Weatherall, H. - Range 4, Township 11 - Colored
   A.W. - male, age 19   Agathie - male, age 9
   M.O. - male, age 10   Gar - male, age 5

Weatherall, H. - Range 4, Township 10 - Colored
   Lonnie - male, age 18

Weatherall, Harry - Range 3, Township 9 - Colored
   Arthur - male, age 17   Golie - female, age 6

Weatherall, Henry - Range 2, Township 11 - Colored
   A.W. - male, age 20

Weatherall, Ike - Guardian - Range 3, Township 9 - Colored
   Prude, Nellie - female, age 12

Weatherall, Jno - Range 3, Township 11 - White
   Jno - male, age 10

Weatherall, Jno - Toccopola - Colored
   Lewis - male, age 10   Susan - female, age 6

Weatherall, Jno - Range 3, Township 11 - Colored
   U.S. - female, age 7   Delta - female, age 5
   Estelle - female, age 7   Mattie - female, age 13

Weatherall, S.R. - Range 2, Township 10 - Colored
   Lou - female, age 12   Pearl - female, age 8

Weatherall, W.A. - Range 3, Township 9 - White
   Josie - female, age 7   Jas - male, age 5

Weatherall, Wesly - Range 3, Township 9 - Colored
   Chas - male, age 12   Robt - male, age 6
   Alex - male, age 10   Prestice - female, age 14
   Ike - male, age 8

Weatherspoon, A.M. - Range 4, Township 9 - Colored
   Ervin - male, age 6   Wm - male, age 11
   Sam - male, age 5   Lewis - male, age 14
   Jno - male, age 8

Weatherspoon, Alex - Range 3, Township 10 - Colored
   Lee - male, age 17   Mat - male, age 13
   Etta - female, age 17   Fred - male, age 12
   Rebecca - female, age 16   Allie - male, age 10
   Judie - female, age 16   Leek - male, age 9
   Walter - male, age 16   Angie - female, age 8
   Mary - female, age 14   Frances - female, age 13

Weatherspoon, H. - Range 4, Township 9 - Colored
   Mollie - female, age 18   Dwight - male, age 12
   Lonnie - male, age 14   Lizzie - female, age 10
   Sam - male, age 15

Weatherspoon, S.M. - Range 4, Township 9 - White
   Alice - female, age 9

Weatherspoon, S.M. - Range 4, Township 9 - Colored
   Jno - male, age 8   Allee - male, age 7

Weaver, N.J. - Range 3, Township 10 - White
   Ida - female, age 20   Bonzell - male, age 9
   Thos - mlae, age 18   Willie - male, age 6
   Jessee - male, age 16   Martha - female, age 5
   Zola - female, age 13

Weaver, W. - Rnge 4, Township 10 - White
   J.T. - female, age 20   Bob - male, age 14
   Chas - male, age 18   Willie - male, age 8
   Jas - male, age 16

Webb, Harvy - Range 4, Township 11 - Colored
   Ester - male, age 7

Webster, J.F. - Range 3, Township 10 - White
   Minnie - female, age 16   Chas - male, age 13

Webster, T.B. - Range 3, Township 10 - White
   Ernest - male, age 11   Rubin - female, age 5
   Bell - female, age 6

Weddon, D.F. - Range 1, Township 9 - White
   Lewis - male, age 8   Willie - male, age 5
   Marion - male, age 5

Weeks, J.M. - Range 3, Township 11 - White
   Bolen - male, age 17   Wm - male, age 13
   Jas - male, age 15   Jones - male, age 10

Wells, C.F. - Range 2, Township 9 - White
   Ollie - female, age 7   Malissa - female, age 5

Wells, J.F. - Range 1, Township 8 - White
   Mattie - female, age 6

Wells, J.P. - Range 1, Township 8 - White
   Sarah - female, age 20   Henry - male, age 11
   George - male, age 15   Jennie - female, age 8
   Mary - female, age 13   Jessie - female, age 5

Wells, M.M. - Range 1, Towsnhip 8 - White
   John - male, age 18   James - male, age 11
   Sallie - female, age 15   Martin - male, age 7
   Emma - female, age 14   Anna - female, age 6

Wells, Tom - Range 1. Township 10 - White
   Dona - female, age 12   Garie - male, age 8
   Lucinda - female, age 10   Ethel - female, age 6

West, J.F. - Range 2, Township 9 - White
   I.M. - male, age 17   Bell - female, age 7
   Nannie - femlae, age 9   Modee - female, age 15

Westmoland, A.J. - Range 1, Township 10 - White
   Andrew - male, age 6

Westmoland, A.W. - Range 1 Township 10 - White
   Martha - female, age 13   Lillie - female, age 9
   Jno - male, age 11

Westmoland, J. - Range 4, Township 9 - White
    Fannie - female, age 19   Maud - female, age 9
    Estelle - female, age 14   Mabel - female, age 6
    Milton - male, age 12

Westmoland, T.J. - Range 1, Township 10 - White
    Jeff - male, age 18   Willis - male, age 14
    Mattie - female, age 17   Artie - female, age 12

Wharton, Richard - Range 4, Township 9 - White
    Earl - male, age 15   Mabel - female, age 10
    Guy - male, age 13   Persie - male, age 6

White, Bale - Range 1, Township 11 - White
    Riley - male, age 12   Jno - male, age 5
    Warren - male, age 7

White, G.E. - Range 1, Township 8 - White
    Estin - male, age 8   Lela - female, age 5

White, G.W. - Range 4, Township 10 - Colored
    Adlena - female, age 11   Thos - male, age 7
    Chas - male, age 9   Mattie - female, age 5

White, H. - Range 1, Township 10 - White
    Donas - female, age 7

White, J.C. - Range 1, Township 10 - White
    Alice - female, age 16   Virginia - female, age 12
    Wm - male, age 14

White, Nancy - Range 3, Township 10 - Colored
    Nathan - male, age 16   John - male, age 13
    Frances - female, age 14

White, Nancy - Range 3, Township 11 - Colored
    Nathan - male, age 16   Frances - female, age 14

White, Reed - Range 4, Township 10 - Colored
    Zack - male, age 15   Millie - female, age 7
    Lillie - female, age 12   Jno - male, age 5
    Pearl - female, age 10

White, T.W. - Range 1, Township 11 - White
    Jennie - female, age 13   Wm - male, age 9
    Ada - female, age 12   Madison - male, age 8
    Mary - female, age 12

White, W.A. - Range 3, Township 10 - White
    Jas - male, age 14   Vallie - female, age 7
    Andrew - male, age 13   Lora - female, age 5
    Willie - male, age 9

White, W.M. - Range 1, Township 8 - White
    Veach - female, age 6   Era - male, age 12

White, Z.E. - Range 1, Township 8 - White
    Wade - male, age 6

Whitesides, W.B. - Toccopola - White
    Lucy - female, age 20

Whitlow, T.W. - Range 4, Township 10 - White
    Jessie - female, age 17   Jettie - female, age 9
    Geo - male, age 15   Wm - male, age 6
    August - male, age 10

Whitlow, W.D. - Range 4, Township 10 - White
    Walter - male, age 18   Jettie - female, age 10
    Bulah - female, age 16   Luther - male, age 7
    Hovelle - female, age 13

Whitten, F.A. - Guardian - Range 4, Township 8 - White
    White, Ed - male, age 9

Whitten, F.A. - Range 4, Township 8 - White
    Nat - male, age 12   Frank - male, age 7
    M - female, age 11   Walter - male, age 5

Whitworth, F.M. - Range 1, Township 10 - White
    Jack - male, age 18   Lizzie - female, age 20
    Ada - female, age 17

Whitworth, M.L. - Range 1, Township 10 - White
    Lee - male, age 16   Artie - female, age 12
    Carry - female, age 15   Dow - male, age 8
    Mattie - female, age 13   Doyle - male, age 6

Whitworth, T.M. - Range 1, Township 11 - White
    Thad - male, age 9   Jane - female, age 5
    Jas - male, age 8

Widener, S.W. - Range 3, Township 9 - White
    Davie - male, age 20   Lollie - female, age 14
    Thos - male, age 18   Lillie - female, age 11

Wilbanks, R.S. - Range 4, Township 9 - White
    Willie - male, age 15   Lula - female, age 8
    Carrie - female, age 12   Carl - male, age 5
    Cora - female, age 8

Wilder, Fannie - Pontotoc - Colored
    Chas - male, age 12   Lillie - female, age 8
    Emma - female, age 12   Sadie - female, age 5

Wilder, L.R. - Range 3, Township 9 - White
    Ida - female, age 17   Etta - female, age 8
    Maggie - female, age 14

Wilder, S.S. - Range 4, Township 10 - White
    Oscar - male, age 11   Bessie - female, age 5
    Chas - male, age 7

Wilder, W.F. - Range 4, Township 9 - White
    Robt - male, age 14   Lila - female, age 9
    Walter - male, age 12   Byron - male. age 5

Wilder, W.H. - RAnge 3, Township 9 - White
    Alma - female, age 6

Wileman, Mack - Range 4, Township 9 - White
    Robt - male, age 16

Wiley, Minnie - Range 4, Township 9 - Colored
    Willie - male, age 8   Frank - male, age 6

Wiley, W.H. - Range 1, Township 9 - White
   James - male, age 20
   Wm - male, age 18
   Daniel - male, age 16
   Mattie - female, age 12
   Hugh - male, age 10
   Lawson - male, age 6

Williams, A.W. - Range 1, Township 8 - White
   Lucinda - female, age 9

Williams, C. - Range 4, Township 10 - Colored
   Albert - male, age 17
   Archie - male, age 15
   Jas - male, age 10
   Lillie - female, age 5

Williams, Dan - Range 3, Township 10 - Colored
   Lula - female, age 9
   Geo - male, age 6
   Lizzie - female, age 14

Williams, E.H. - Range 3, Township 9 - White
   Ditzler - male, age 16
   Proctor - male, age 8
   Lillian - female, age 10

Williams, Essex - Range 2, Township 11 - Colored
   Lee - male, age 11
   Gabe - male, age 9

Williams, Geo - Range 4, Township 10 - Colored
   Augusta - male, age 16
   Lewis - male, age 13
   Addie - female, age 11
   Joe - male, age 6
   Dan'l - male, age 5

Williams, Gus - Range 3, Township 10 - Colored
   Gus - male, age 16
   Lewis - male, age 13
   Addie - female, age 11
   Joe - male, age 8
   Jno - male, age 6
   Daniel - male, age 5

Williams, Isaac - Range 3, Township 10 - Colored
   Cetera - female, age 17
   Jno - male, age 16
   Willie - male, age 12
   Isaac - male, age 10
   Pauline - female, age 8

Williams, J.G. - Range 1, Township 10 - White
   Gilbert - male, age 18
   Jas - male, age 16
   Castilla - female, age 15
   May - female, age 13
   Lizzie - female, age 12
   Jno - male, age 10
   Peyton - male, age 8
   Minnie - female, age 7
   Jack - male, age 5

Williams, J.T. - Range 4, Township 11 - White
   J.T. - male, age 19
   M.I. - female, age 18
   W.C. - male, age 16
   E.J. - male, age 14
   Mattie - female, age 12
   J.L. - male, age 11
   J.C. - male, age 12

Williamson, M.E. - Pontotoc - White
   Hassie - female, age 19
   Ida - female, age 18
   Jas - male, age 14
   Memory - male, age 10

Williams, Manda - Range 4, Township 11 - Colored
   Abe - male, age 20

Williams, N.C. - Range 4, Township 11 - White
   Frank - male, age 20
   Nora - female, age 18
   Birdie - female, age 14
   Lewis - male, age 10
   Bell, Willie - female, age 14

Williams, Robt - Range 3, Township 10 - Colored
    Robt - male, age 18   Pias - male, age 8
    Wm - male, age 17   Desseratte - male, age 7
    Lula - femlae, age 14   Menail - female, age 6
    Anna - female, age 10

Williams, T.H. - Range 3, Township 11 - White
    Lou - female, age 19   Mary - female, age 15

Wileman, Jane - Range 3, Township 10 - Colored
    Lizzie - female, age 18   Dice - female, age 8
    Wm - male, age 16   Linda - female, age 5
    Peggy - female, age 13

Wingo, J.T. - Toccopola - White
    Madden - male, age 10   Golden - male, age 6
    Perry - male, age 8

Wilson, Allen - Pototoc - Colored
    Jno - male, age 12   Wm - male, age 7

Wilson, G.B. - Range 4, Township 9 - White
    Willie - male, age 16   Abner - male, age 10
    Ada - female, age 14   Maud - female, age 5
    Myrtie - female, age 13

Wilson, G.W. - Range 4, Township 10 - White
    Wm - male, age 11   P.D. - male, age 7
    Minnie - female, age 9   Harriett - female, age 6

Wilson, Jane - Range 2, Township 10 - Colored
    Sam - male, age 13

Wilson, Joe - Range 3, Township 9 - White
    Lee - male, age 18

Wilson, Mrs. E.J. - Range 3, Township 10 - White
    Sallie - female, age 20

Wilson, Robert - Guardian - Range 3, Township 9 - Colored
    Montgomery, Maggie - female, age 16   Hyde, Minor - male, age 12
    Hyde, James - male, age 13   Hyde, Antney - male, age 18
    Hyde, Addie - female, age 18

Wilson, T.B. - Range 3, Township 9 - White
    James - male, age 7

Wilson, W.M. - Range 2, Towsnhip 10 - White
    Demie - female, age 19   Rushie - female, age 12
    Callis - female, age 18   Myrtis - female, age 9
    Joe - male, age 14

Wilson, Wm - Guardian - Range 3, Township 9 - Colored
    Payne, Henry - male, age 17

Winders, W.H. - Range 3, Township 8 - White
    Barley - male, age 13   Rona - female, age 11

Windham, P.J. - Range 2, Township 11 - White
    M.M. - female, age 20   John - male, age 14
    Mattie - female, age 19   F.A. - female, age 10
    Willie - male, age 17   Robt - male, age 8
    Jane - female, age 16

Wingo, H.C. - Range 2, Township 10 - White
   Willie - male, age 6

Wingo, T.J. - Range 1, Township 10 - White
   Madden - male, age 10   Galen - male, age 6
   Perry - male, age 8

Winfield, J.B. - Range 4, Township 9 - White
   Andrew - male, 7   Smith, Joe - male, age 10
   Smith, Willie - male, age 12

Winfield, R.G. - Range 4, Township 9 - White
   Rachael - female, age 15

Winson, Mrs. E.E. - Range 3, Township 9 - White
   E.T. - male, age 20   Mamie - female, age 16

Winter, Wm - Range 3, Township 11 - White
   Lon - male, age 9   Addie - female, age 7

Wise, Tom - Range 1, Township 8 - White
   Early - female, age 10   Vannah - female, age 7
   Rilla - female, age 8

Witt, J.M. - Range 4, Township 8 - White
   Thos - male, age 16   Etta - female, age 9
   James - male, age 14   Chas - male, age 7

Witt, W.A. - Range 4, Township 8 - White
   Jno - mlae, age 19   Chas - male, age 10
   Rad - male, age 15   Ben - male, age 7
   Andrew - male, age 12   Ara - female, age 17

Witt, W.R. - Range 4, Township 8 - White
   Lee - male, age 6   Lillie - female, age 8
   Martha - female, age 12

Wooley, J.L. - Range 4, Township 9 - White
   Victoria - female, age 19   Geo - male, age 14

Wood, C. - Range 3, Township 10 - Colored
   Fred - male, age 5

Wood, Calvin - Range 3, Township 9 - Colored
   Fred - male, age 5

Wood, E.W. - Range 3, Township 9 - Colored
   Wiley - male, age 8   Onie - female, age 5
   Lena - female, age 6

Wood, J.T. - Range 1, Township 9 - White
   Sila - female, age 16   Corra - female, age 14

Wood, J.T. - Guardian - Range 1, Township 9 - White
   Joyner, David - male, age 19   Joyner, Dora - female, age 11
   Joyner, James - male, age 17   Joyner, Henry - male, age 12
   Joyner, Laura - female, age 15   Joyner, Joe - male, age 10
   Joyner, Burrell - male, age 14   Joyner, Tom - male, age 8

Wood, Jennie - Range 4, Township 10 - Colored
   Julia - female, age 17   Isaac - male, age 12
   Ida - female, age 15   Jake - male, age 5

Wood, Mrs. Sallie - Range 2, Township 10 - White
   Carrie - female, age 5

Wood, R.D. - Range 3, Township 10 - White
   Allie - female, age 18   Lonnie - male, age 12
   Rilla - female, age 6   Booker - male, age 8
   Ollie - male, age 14

Wood, W.H. - Pontotoc - White
   Frank - male, age 8   May - female, age 6

Wood, W.J. - Range 2, Township 10 - White
   Maggie - male, age 5

Wood, W.W. - Range 2, Township 10 - White
   Mattie - female, age 19   Mary - female, age 12
   Birdie - female, age 17   Walter - male, age 10
   Lewis - male, age 14   Willie - male, age 6

Wood, Wm - Range 3, Township 11 - White
   Martha - female, age 16   Jack - male, age 9
   Sallie - female, age 12   Mamie - female, age 15
   Albert - male, age 8

Woodard, Evans - Range 3, Township 10 - Colored
   Anna - female, age 6

Woods, Richard - Range 2, Township 11 - Colored
   Joe - male, age 8   Albert - male, age 5

Wooley, Mrs. Mollie - Range 4, Townshp 10 - White
   Gy - male, age 14   A.A. - male, age 20

Wooten, J.L. - Toccopola - White
   Jno - male, age 19   J.B. - male, age 14

Wooten, T.L. - Range 3, Township 9 - White
   Wm - male, age 13   Annie - female, age 9
   Chas - male, age 12   Archie - male, age 6

Word, J.H. - Range 2, Township 9 - White
   Barney - male, age 11

Wordlaw, Sallie - Range 3, Township 10 - Colored
   Lizzie - female, age 17   Early - male, age 15
   Georgia - female, age 18   Estelle - female, age 15

Worsham, J.M. - Range 4, Township 11 - White
   Genl - male, age 16   Jennie - female, age 12
   Col - male, age 15   Judge - male, age 19

Wray, C.M. - Range 2, Township 9 - White
   Addie - female, age 8

Wray, J.F. - Range 3, Township 10 - White
   M.J. - male, age 18

Wright, L. - Range 3, Township 8 - Colored
   Pink - male, age 18   Jeff - male, age 12
   Antoney - male, age 14   Lena - female, age 9

Wright, Melton - Range 3, Township 9 - Colored
   Azzie - male, age 17   Richard - male, age 10
   Peter - male, age 14   Earnest - male, age 8
   Arthur - male, age 12   Sarah - female, age 6

York, J.M. - Range 1, Township 9 - White
   Walter - male, age 15   Curtis - male, age 8
   Earnest - male, age 12

Young, A.C. - Range 1, Township 11 - White
   Jane - female, age 15   Julia - female, age 8
   Henry - male, age 13   George - male, age 6
   John - male, age 11

Young, Anna - Pontotoc - Colored
   Lou - femlae, age 7   Elias - male, age 5

Young, Eli - Guardian - Range 3, Township 10 - Colored
   Hare, Lela - female, age 6

Young, Elias - Range 4, Township 11 - Colored
   James - male, age 19   Leatha - female, age 12
   Emison - male age 19   Earl - male, age 11
   Lela - female, age 16   Cassie - female, age 9
   John - male, age 14   Dee - male, age 7
   Clarence - male, age 13   Jane - female, age 5

Young, Green - Range 3, Township 9 - Colored
   Wm - male, age 11   Hannah - female, age 8

Young, J.A. - Range 4, Township 10 - White
   G.W. - male, age 15   Etta - female, age 11
   M.L. - male, age 13

Yount, Mrs. F.L. - Range 3, Township 10 - White
   J.E. - male, age 18   Susan - female, age 7
   W.T. - male, age 15   Smith, M.E. - female, age 17
   A.B. - male, age 13   Smith, S.E. - female, age 13
   A.A. - female, age 13

Zachary, T. - Range 1, Township 11 - White
   Robert - male, age 19   John - male, age 12
   Ira - male, age 15   Given - male, age 7
   Wash - male, age 14   Edna - female, age 6

Zinn, Fayette - Range 1, Township 11 - Colored
   Leland - male, age 6

Zinn, Thos - Range 1, Township 11 - White
   Thomas - male, age 10   Thester - male, age 5
   Mamie - female, age 8

RECAPITULATION

WHITE MALES	2335		**COLORED MALES**	942
WHITE FEMALES	2220		**COLORED FEMALES**	742
TOTAL	4555		**TOTAL**	1682

GRAND TOTAL - 6237

FILED AUGUST 1ST 1892
T.A. BRAMLETT
CHANCERY CLERK

www.ingramcontent.com/pod-product-compliance
Lightning Source LLC
Chambersburg PA
CBHW080551170426
43195CB00016B/2750